Parents Guide

to the

Internet

By Jay LaBonte

To my wife Kathy
and my three children
Andrew, Gianna and Jack.

Table of Contents

Introduction

This is not a book about networking, or how to setup your computer. It's about what parents need to know before they let their kids loose on the internet.

The idea for this book came to me while watching various television shows about sexual predators. Interview after interview, parents were saying the same thing, "I don't know much about the internet", or "My kids know a lot more about computers than I do!"

I realized at this point, that unless you are a computer professional, or network engineer, or a corporate network security professional, most kids these days have the advantage.

Since I have been involved with information technology for over 36 years, I instinctively understand what dangers await children on the internet. I know what is needed to protect my own children online.

Unfortunately, not everyone has access to that knowledge, and in most cases are impressed that their children understand the technology.

This book will explain what the internet is, what applications, and hardware are used to explore the internet.

At some point your child/teen will come to you and tell you that they need a Gigabit Ethernet switch, or a new router, or an 802.11g PCMCIA card. You may be impressed that they know what these things are, and may not want to question them about it, so this book should help answer some questions.

This book is designed to educate yourself, so you know what your children are talking about.

Statistics

Children and teens are at a higher risk to be victims of Internet crimes than most parents realize. It is important that parents understand the scope of the problem, to identify the benefits of childhood Internet activity and where your child may be in danger online.

By the end of 1998, more than 40 percent of all American homes had computers, and 25 percent had Internet access. This trend is expected to continue. Children and teenagers are one of the fastest growing groups of Internet users. An estimated 78 million children and teens are online today.

- The Center for Missing and Exploited Children states only 1/3 of the households with Internet access are proactively protecting their children with filtering or blocking software.

- The eMarketer claims 75 percent of children are willing to share personal information online about themselves and their family in exchange for goods and services.

- According to the Youth Internet Safety Survey, only about 25 percent of the youth who encountered a sexual approach or solicitation told a parent.

- The Crimes Against Children Research Center claims one in five U.S. teenagers who regularly log on to the Internet say they have received an unwanted sexual solicitation via the Web. Solicitations were defined as requests to engage in sexual activities or sexual talk, or to give personal sexual information.

- The Youth Internet Safety Survey found that one in 33 youth received an aggressive sexual solicitation in the past year. This means a predator asked a young person to meet somewhere, called a young person on the phone, and/or sent the young person correspondence, money, or gifts through the U.S. Postal Service.

- The Crimes against Children Research Center found that 77 percent of the targets for online predators were age 14 or older. Another 22 percent were users ages 10 to 13.

- 75 percent of the solicited youth were not troubled, 10 percent did not use chat rooms and 9 percent did not talk to strangers according to the Crimes against Children Research Center.

- Crimes against Children Research Center found that only 25 percent of solicited children were distressed by their encounters and told a parent.

- Only 17 percent of youth and 11 percent of parents could name a specific authority to which they could report an Internet crime.

The Internet

The Internet, or simply the Net, is the publicly accessible worldwide system of interconnected computer networks that transmit data by packet switching using a standardized Internet Protocol (IP). It is made up of thousands of smaller commercial, academic, domestic, and government networks. It carries various information and services, such as electronic mail, online chat, and the interlinked Web pages and other documents of the World Wide Web.

Contrary to some common usage, the Internet and the World Wide Web are not synonymous: the Internet is a collection of interconnected computer networks, linked by copper wires, fiber-optic cables, wireless connections etc.; the Web is a collection of interconnected documents, linked by hyperlinks and Uniform Resource Locator (URL). A URL is simple a path to a document or page on the web, and is accessible using the Internet.

History

On October 4th, 1957, the Union of Soviet Socialist Republic (USSR) launched the first man made satellite named Sputnik. Sputnik spurred the United State to create the

Defense Advanced Research Projects Agency (DARPA) in February 1958 to regain a technological lead. DARPA created the Information Processing Technology Office (IPTO) to further the research of the Semi-automatic Ground Environment program, which had networked country-wide radar systems together for the first time. J.C.R. Licklider was selected to head the IPTO, and saw universal networking as a potential unifying human revolution. Licklider recruited Lawrence Roberts to head a project to implement a network, and Roberts based the technology on the work of Paul Baran who had written an exhaustive study for the U.S. Air Force that recommended packet switching to make a network highly robust and survivable. After much work, the first node went live at UCLA on October 29, 1969 on what would be called the ARPANET, which eventually would become the network of today's Internet.

In December of 1970, Charles A. Petrik contacted the U.S. Navy and suggested that a special communications network, that the Department of Defense had built for use in the possibility of a nuclear attack, could also be used during peace time. Petrik convinced the military to connect the computers of the U.S. National Laboratories for scientific research purposes, and to allow these labs to get data to other labs faster, and safer.

The first Transmission Control Protocol (TCP) based wide area network was operational by January 1st, 1983, when the United States' National Science Foundation (NSF) constructed a university network backbone that would later become the NSFNet. This date is held by some to be technically that of the birth of the Internet. It was then followed by the opening of the network to commercial interests in 1995. Important separate networks that offered gateways into, and then later merged into the Internet include Usenet, Bitnet and the various commercial and educational X.25 networks such as CompuServe and JANET. The ability of TCP/IP to work over these pre-existing communication networks allowed for a great ease of growth. Use of Internet as a phrase to describe a single global TCP/IP network originated around this time.

The network gained a public face in the 1990s. In August 1991 CERN, which straddles the border between France and Switzerland publicized the new World Wide Web project, two years after Tim Berners-Lee had begun creating HTML, HTTP and the first few web pages at CERN, which was set up by international treaty and not bound by the laws of either France or Switzerland. In 1993 the National Center for Supercomputing Applications at the University of Illinois at Urbana-Champaign released the Mosaic web browser version 1.0, and by late 1994 there was growing public interest in the previously academic/technical Internet. By 1996 the word "Internet" was common public currency, but it referred almost entirely to the World Wide Web.

Meanwhile, over the course of the decade, the Internet successfully accommodated the majority of previously existing public computer networks, although some networks such as FidoNet have remained separate. This growth is often attributed to the lack of central administration, which allows organic growth of the network, as well as the non-proprietary open nature of the Internet protocols, which encourages vendor interoperability and prevents any one company from exerting too much control over the network.

Today's Internet

Aside from the complex physical connections that make up its infrastructure, the Internet is held together by multi-lateral commercial contracts and by technical specifications or protocols that describe how to exchange data over the network. Indeed, the Internet is essentially defined by its interconnections and routing policies.

As of January 2006, over 1 billion people use the Internet according to Internet World Statistics.

Internet protocols

Exchange of information over the internet, as well as most private networks, is regulated using standardized protocols. These protocols determine how data will be exchanged. These define how programs will start a conversation or handshake with each other, how to handle errors, and how to say goodbye.

In the context of the internet, there are three layers of protocols:

At the first level is Internet Protocol (IP), which defines the datagram's or packets that carry blocks of data from one node to another. The vast majority of today's Internet uses version 4 of the IP protocol (IPv4), and although Internet

Protocol version 6 (IPv6), has been standardized, it exists only as islands of connectivity, and there are many Internet Service Providers (ISPs), who don't have any IPv6 connectivity at all.

At the second level are the Transmission Control Protocol (TCP) and User Datagram Protocol (UDP). These are the protocols by which one computer sends data to another. TCP makes a virtual connection, which gives some level of guarantee of reliability, while UDP is a best-effort, connection-less transport, in which data packets that are lost in transmission will not be re-sent.

At the third or top level comes the application protocol. This defines the specific messages and data formats sent and understood by the applications running at each end of the communication.

Unlike older communications systems, the Internet protocol suite was deliberately designed to be independent of the underlying physical medium. Any communications network, wired or wireless, that can carry two-way digital data can carry Internet traffic. Thus, Internet packets flow through wired networks like copper wire, coaxial cable, and fiber optic, and through wireless networks like Wi-Fi. Together, all these networks sharing the same protocols form the Internet.

The Internet protocols originate from discussions within the Internet Engineering Task Force (IETF) and its working groups, which are open to public participation and review. These committees produce documents that are known as Request for Comments documents (RFCs). Some RFCs are raised to the status of Internet Standard by the IETF process.

Some of the most-used application protocols in the Internet protocol suite are DNS, POP3, IMAP, SMTP, HTTP, HTTPS and FTP. There are many other important ones; see the lists provided in these articles.

All services on the Internet make use of defined application protocols. Of these, e-mail and the World Wide Web are among the most well known, and other services are built upon these, such as mailing lists and blogs. There are many others that are necessary 'behind the scenes' and yet others that serve specialized requirements.

Some application protocols were not created out of the IETF process, but initially as part of proprietary commercial or private experimental systems. They became much more widely used and have now become de facto or actual standards in their own right. Examples of these include IRC chat rooms, and various instant messaging and peer-to-peer file sharing protocols.

Below is a brief explanation of the internet protocols mentioned above:

- **DNS** - Domain Name Server is a system that stores and associates many types of information with domain names, but most important, it translates the domain name or computer hostnames to IP addresses.

- **SMTP** - Simple Mail Transfer Protocol is the de facto standard for e-mail and internet fax transmissions across the Internet.

- **POP3** - Post Office Protocol version 3, is an application-layer Internet standard protocol, to retrieve e-mail from a remote server over a TCP/IP connection. Nearly all subscribers to individual Internet service provider e-mail accounts access their e-mail with client software that uses POP3.

- **IMAP** - Internet Message Access Protocol is an application layer Internet protocol that allows a local client to access e-mail on a remote server. IMAP and POP3 are the most commonly used protocols used for email exchange.

- **HTTP** - Hypertext Transfer Protocol is the method used to transfer or convey information on the World Wide Web.

- **HTTPS** - Hypertext Transfer Protocol Secure is syntactically identical to the http scheme normally used for accessing resources on the web, except HTTPS used encryption for secure transfer of data.

- **FTP** - File Transfer Protocol is a commonly used protocol for exchanging files over any network that supports the TCP/IP protocol.

13

Domain Names

A domain name usually consists of two or more parts separated by dots. For example 'safecheckcorp.com'

The rightmost label conveys the top-level domain. For example, the address 'mail.safecheckcorp.com' has the top-level domain 'com'.

Each label to the left specifies a subdivision or subdomain of the domain above it. Note that "subdomain" expresses relative dependence, not absolute dependence: for example, safecheckcorp.com comprises a subdomain of the 'com' domain, and 'mail.safecheckcorp.com' comprises a subdomain of the domain 'safecheckcorp.com'. In theory, this subdivision can go down to 127 levels deep, and each label can contain up to 63 characters, as long as the whole domain name does not exceed a total length of 255 characters. But in practice some domain registries have shorter limits than that.

Remote Access

The Internet allows computer users to connect to other computers and information stores easily, wherever they may be across the world. Internet user may access countless systems with or without the use of security, user authentication or encryption technologies, depending on the requirements.

Through remote access, users are encouraged to find new ways of working from home, collaboration and information sharing in many industries. An accountant sitting at home can audit the books of a company based in another country, on a server situated in a third country that is remotely maintained by IT specialists in a fourth country. These accounts could have been created by home-working bookkeepers, in other remote locations, based on information e-mailed to them from offices all over the world. Some of these things were possible before the widespread use of the Internet, but the cost of private, leased lines would have made many of them infeasible in practice.

An office worker away from his desk, perhaps the other side of the world on a business trip or a holiday, can open a remote desktop session into his normal office PC using a secure Virtual Private Network (VPN) connection via the Internet. This gives him complete access to all his normal files and data, including e-mail and other applications, while he is away.

Internet Access

Common methods of home access include dial-up, landline broadband (over coaxial cable, fiber optic or copper wires), Wi-Fi, satellite and cell phones.

Public places to use the Internet include libraries and Internet cafes, where computers with Internet connections are available. There are also Internet access points in many public places like airport halls, in some cases just for brief use while standing. Various terms are used, such as "public Internet kiosk", "public access terminal", and "Web payphone". Many hotels now also have public terminals, though these are usually fee based.

Wi-Fi provides wireless access to computer networks, and therefore can do so to the Internet itself. Hotspots providing such access include Wi-Fi cafes, where a would-be user needs to bring their own wireless-enabled devices such as a laptop or PDA. These services may be free to all, free to customers only, or fee-based. A hotspot need not be limited to a confined location. The whole campus or park, or even the entire city can be enabled. Grassroots efforts have led to wireless community networks. Commercial Wi-Fi services covering large city areas are in place in London, San Francisco, Philadelphia, Chicago, and other cities. The Internet can then be accessed from such places as a park bench.

Internet Service Providers

An Internet service provider (ISP), also called Internet access provider (IAP) is a business or organization that offers users access to the Internet and related services. Many but not all ISP's are telephone companies. They provide services such as Internet transit, domain name registration, Web site hosting, and dial-up or DSL access to the Internet.

ISP connection options

Generally, an ISP charges a monthly access fee to the consumer. The consumer then has access to the Internet, although the speed at which this data is transferred varies widely.

Internet connection speed can generally be divided into two categories: dialup and broadband. The speed that these connects communicate are measured in kilobits (kb) or megabits (mb). A kilobit is the equivalent of 1024 bits of information, while a megabit is 1,024,000 bits of information. It takes 8 bits to transmit a single character of byte of information. For example, the word "hello" consists of 5 bytes, and each byte contains 8 bits, so the word "hello" is 40 bits.

Dialup connections require the use of a phone line, and usually have connections of 56-kilobits or less. Broadband connections can be either Broadband wireless access, Cable modem, DSL, Fiber Optics, or Satellite. Broadband is an always on connection, and varies in speed between 64-kilobits and 6-megabits per second or more.

With the increasing popularity of file sharing and downloading music and the general demand for faster page loads, higher bandwidth connections are becoming more popular.

Broadband

Digital Subscriber Line (DSL), is a family of technologies that provide digital data transmission over the wires used in the "last mile" of a local telephone network. The download speed of DSL ranges from 128 kilobits per second to 2 megabits per second, depending on DSL technology and service level implemented. Upload speed is lower than download speed for Asymmetric Digital Subscriber Line (ADSL) and equal to download speed for Symmetric Digital Subscriber Line (SDSL).

Broadband also covers cable modems which have high data-transmission rates ranging from 256 kilobits per second or more, starting at approximately four times the speed of a standard dialup modem using a telephone line.

Legal Issues

The internet posses many legal issues, since the internet is not owned by any one country, and no country or government controls it, each country is responsible for enforcing its own laws in its own country.

Unfortunately some countries have very few laws governing the Internet. What is illegal in one country may be legal in another country.

The Children's Online Privacy Protection Act

The primary goal of the Children's Online Privacy Protection Act (COPPA) Rule is to give parents control over what information is collected from their children online and how such information may be used.

The Rule applies to:

- Operators of commercial Web sites and online services directed to children 13 and under that collect personal information from them;

- Operators of general audience sites that knowingly collect personal information from children 13 and under; and

- Operators of general audience sites that have a separate children's area and that collect personal information from children 13 and under.

The Rule requires operators to:
- Post a privacy policy on the homepage of the Web site and link to the privacy policy on every page where personal information is collected.

- Provide notice about the site's information collection practices to parents and obtain verifiable parental consent before collecting personal information from children.

- Give parents a choice as to whether their child's personal information will be disclosed to third parties.

- Provide parents access to their child's personal information and the opportunity to delete the child's personal information and opt-out of future collection or use of the information.

- Operators can not require a child to disclose more personal information than is reasonably necessary to participate in a game, contest or other activity. This information is generally limited to name and age.

- Maintain the confidentiality, security and integrity of personal information collected from children.

In order to encourage active industry self-regulation, COPPA also includes a safe harbor provision allowing industry groups and others to request Commission approval of self-regulatory guidelines to govern participating Web sites' compliance with the Rule.

Child Porn

At a press conference in Washington, D.C., the International Center for Missing and Exploited Children and other participants including Microsoft presented a study that reveals the woeful inadequacy of child pornography laws around the world.

The ICMEC's global policy review of child pornography laws in 184 Interpol-member countries shows that more than half have no laws that specifically address child pornography and in many other countries the existing laws are insufficient.

As a result, it is difficult to eliminate illegal Internet content, because the servers are connected to the Internet, and are hosted in countries where the content does not violate any laws.

The ICMEC study found that possession of child pornography is not a crime in 138 countries. In 122 countries, there are no laws dealing with the use of computers and the Internet as a means of child porn distribution.

Internet Gambling

Many children search the internet looking for games and other entertainment. They generally find all types of games, from card games to board games, to arcade type games.

Sometimes they come across gaming sites where they can play various casino type games and win or lose some form of artificial money.

The problem with these types of gaming sites is that they prepare children to gamble. They get used to playing these games online, and as a result they naturally progress to gambling.

Many of the gaming sites that use artificial money are often operated by the same people that run the on-line gambling sites. The primary difference is that the gaming sites are designed to allow the player to win. This causes the player to think he's good at the games, and pushes him to try the gambling sites, thinking his new found luck will make him rich.

The gambling sites generally favor the site operators, and the child quickly begins to lose. Thinking his luck will change, he quickly becomes addicted to trying to win. He doesn't equate gambling to the loss of money, because he never sees the money. To a child gambler, it's just a method of keeping score.

The National Research Council (NRC) claims most children that gamble are between the ages of 10 to 20, and nearly 6 percent of them gamble, and have gambled recently.

The most common types of gambling for children are reported to be card games and sports betting. Since many of the game operators are operating from servers outside of the United States, they are beyond the jurisdiction of state or federal regulations that normally regulate the hours of operation, the age of the participants, or the types of games offered.

According to the Federal Trade Commission (FTC), it's easy for children to access online gambling sites, especially if they have access to credit or debit cards.

Children and parents together must understand the risks associated with gambling online:

- You will lose your money. Online gambling operations are in business to make a profit. They take in more money than they pay out.

- You can ruin a good credit rating. Online gambling generally requires the use of a credit card. If children rack up debt online, they could ruin their credit rating or their parents by using their credit card. That can prevent you from getting a loan to buy a house or a car, or even from getting a job.

- Online gambling can be addictive. Internet gambling is a solitary activity, people can gamble uninterrupted and undetected for hours at a time. Gambling in social isolation and using credit to gamble are risk factors for developing gambling problems. Gamblers Anonymous is a self-help group for problem gamblers.

- Gambling is illegal for kids. Every state prohibits gambling by minors. Unfortunately there are gambling sites outside the U.S. that regularly ignore these laws, and have very limited age verification if any. Most of the time the age verification process simply requires the user to click on a button acknowledging that they are over the age of 18.

Here are some easy steps to help you prevent minors from logging on and gambling:

- Use child protection software to block gaming sites.

- Do not share your credit card or bank account details with your children.

23

- Create separate profiles for your children on the family computer, so that when they log in they cannot access your information.

Tools of the Internet

As we discussed earlier, the internet is nothing more that a network of interconnected computers and smaller networks of computers. In its native form, the Internet doesn't offer much other than potential.

To really do anything on the Internet, you need to use software tools. These tools allow you to exchange information, format information, distribute it, and manage it.

Explained here are some of the more common tools used on the Internet.

The World Wide Web

Internet Explorer is a software program to access the massive amounts of information on the World Wide Web.

Search engines like Google, and Yahoo, allow you to have access to millions of documents, web pages and photos with simple keyword-driven searches.

Compared to encyclopedias and traditional libraries, the World Wide Web has enabled a sudden and extreme decentralization of information and data.

Some companies and individuals have adopted the use of "weblogs" or "blogs", which are largely used as easily-updatable online diaries.

Email

Electronic mail, abbreviated e-mail or email, is a method of composing, sending, and receiving messages over electronic communication systems.

E-mail started in 1965 as a way for multiple users of a time-sharing mainframe computer to communicate, and played an important role in creating the Internet.

As networking computer systems expanded, E-mail also expanded to become network e-mail, allowing users to pass messages between different computers.

Chat Rooms

A chat room is an online forum where people can chat online (talk by broadcasting messages to people on the same forum in real time). Sometimes these venues are moderated either by limiting who is allowed to speak (not common), or by having moderation volunteers patrol the venue watching for disruptive or otherwise undesirable behavior.

Chat systems come in a variety of styles ranging from text only messaging systems to fully immersive 3D environments. By far the most common form in recent times is instant messaging (ICQ, AIM, MSN, Jabber, etc). Some would argue that these are not truly chat rooms as they are characterized by being one on one conversation with people in a users "buddy list". However as the popular media has confused the issue, this brief description is included here. Recently these systems have started to incorporate the ability to chat with multiple people simultaneously, but these are still conversations restricted to the users buddy list, not a cocktail/block party style venue as true chat rooms are.

According to the National Research Council (NRC), about 90 percent of users who frequently use chat rooms are male, this figure does not account for males who claim to be females, which is a fairly common act.

The oldest form of true chat rooms is the text-based variety. The most popular of this kind of chat room is Internet Relay Chat or IRC. However, there are many other publicly available chat systems, while others are private. The popularity of many of these kinds of chat rooms has waned over the years, but IRC's popularity still remains strong.

At the next level are the 2D visual chat rooms. These are characterized by using a graphic representation of the user called an avatar that can be moved about a graphic background of the "room". Two examples of this type of chat room are "The Palace" and more recently "The Manor". These environments are capable of incorporating elements such as games and educational material most often developed by individual site owners, who in general are simply more advanced users of the systems. Some visual chat rooms also incorporate audio and video communications, so that users may actually see and hear each other.

Finally, there are the 3D chat rooms. These are similar to the 2D variety except that they utilize 3D graphics. This allows a user a more realistic interaction with the environment. The most popular environments allow users to create or "build" their own spaces. However, some find these types of environments cumbersome to use and actually an impediment to chatting. Two examples of this type of chat are, "www.activeworlds.com", and "secondlife.com".

Some people who visit chat rooms use them as a place to experience online sex, also known as cybersex. While not physically able to see their partner, cyber-ers apparently get stimulation by reading x-rated quotes. While many in the media focus on this aspect of chat rooms as it certainly boosts their ratings, it is by no means the only thing chat rooms are used for.

Chat rooms have become the new hunting ground for pedophiles, and rapists. By pretending to be a child they can quickly begin chatting with many prospective victims on-line. By pretending to be children, pedophiles can often extract information from unsuspecting children that they can later use to abduct the child.

Children are very trusting and may quickly dish out information that they feel is safe, but in the wrong hands can be life threatening. With as little as a name, grade and school name, a pedophile can easily locate a child.

Instant Messenger

Instant messaging is the act of instantly communicating between two or more people over a network such as the Internet.

Instant messaging requires the use of a client program that connects to an instant messaging service and differs from e-mail in that conversations are then able to happen in real-time. Most services offer a presence information feature, indicating whether people on one's list of contacts are currently online and available to chat. This may be called a 'Buddy List'.

Popular instant messaging services on the public Internet include Qnext, MSN Messenger, AOL Instant Messenger, Yahoo! Messenger, Skype, Google Talk, .NET Messenger Service, Jabber, QQ, iChat and ICQ.

IRC

Internet Relay Chat or IRC is a form of instant communication over the Internet. It is mainly designed for group communication in discussion forums called channels, but also allows one-to-one communication.

IRC has evolved over the years to allow many other information exchanges including MP3, gaming and peer-to-peer chat.

Peer-to-peer chatting's largest concern is that it allows two users to directly connect to each others computer and chat, and exchange photos, and any other file, in total privacy.

ICQ

ICQ is an instant messaging program owned by AOL, and is similar to AOL's Instant Messenger. The name ICQ is a play on the phrase "I seek you".

Due to the lack of security and filtering, the ICQ policy states that they do not allow anyone under the age of 13 to use their chat services. The policy is to terminate anyone's ICQ account if they learn that the user is under the age of 13.

Unfortunately the ICQ service does not verify the age or identity of its users, and anyone, regardless of age, including a child, can give the ICQ service false information including age, with little to no chance of being detected.

The ICQ service is divided into channels, with each channel having a specific topic. These topics can range from "Board and want to chat" or "20 something" to "Girls seeking girls" or "Gay chat".

Blogs

A weblog (usually shortened to blog, but occasionally spelled web log or weblog) is a web-based publication consisting primarily of periodic articles, normally in reverse chronological order. Although most early weblogs were manually updated, tools to automate the maintenance of such sites made them accessible to a much larger population, and the use of some sort of browser-based software is now a typical aspect of "blogging".

Blogs often focus on a particular subject, such as food, music, politics, or local news. Some blogs function as online diaries. A typical blog combines text, images, and links to other blogs, web pages, and other media related to its topic.

Myspace.com is one of the more popular blog hosting sites, and has become very popular with children ages 12 to 20. These children create very detailed blogs about them-selves for the benefit of their friends at school. Older teens and college students tend to use the site to keep in touch with high school friends.

As a result pedophiles have found sites like my MySpace.com to be a fertile hunting ground for victims. Children tend to post very personal information, thoughts, and photos on their blog, thinking only their friends will see it. Pedophile can use this information to befriend the child and gain their trust, knowing that this is the age when most children are at odds with their parents. The pedophile sud-denly appears as the adult that "understands" them.

Vlogs

A vlog or video blog is a blog which uses video as the primary content; the video is linked to within a videoblog post and usually accompanied by supporting text, images, and additional information to provide context.

Video-blogging is rising in popularity, especially since the release of the new Apple Video iPod which can store and play video content. This has resulted in many other companies producing similar portable devices that play video.

One of the potential problems with Vlogs is the current inability of search engines and internet filtering software to determine the content of the video, and filter it as needed.

Therefore anyone can easily post a pornographic video on a video-blog that has been designed to lure children. Video-blogs may contain captions referencing a child's favorite cartoon, or superhero, but once the child gets to the site and downloads the video content to his iPod, he quickly finds out it's a pornographic video.

Wiki's

A wiki is a type of website that allows users to easily add, remove, or otherwise edit all content, very quickly and easily. This ease of interaction and operation makes a wiki an effective tool for collaborative writing. The term Wiki can also refer to the collaborative software itself that facilitates the operation of such a website.

Wiki is sometimes interpreted as an acronym for "What I know is", which describes the knowledge contribution, storage and exchange of information for which a Wiki is designed.

In essence, a wiki is a simplification of the process of creating web pages combined with a system that records each individual change that occurs over time, so that at any time, a page can be reverted to any of its previous states. A wiki system may also include various tools, designed to provide users with an easy way to monitor the constantly changing state of the wiki as well as a place to discuss and resolve the many inevitable issues, namely, the inherent disagreement over wiki content. Wiki content can also be misleading, as users are bound to add incorrect information to the wiki page.

Most wiki's will allow completely unrestricted access so that people are able to contribute to the site without necessarily having to undergo a process of 'registration', as had usually been required by various other types of interactive websites such as Internet forums or chat sites.

A wiki enables documents to be written collectively in a very simple markup language using a web browser. A single page in a wiki is referred to as a "wiki page", whilst the entire body of pages, which are usually highly interconnected via hyperlinks, is "the wiki"; in effect, a wiki is a very simple, easy-to-use user-maintained database for searching information.

A defining characteristic of wiki technology is the ease with which pages can be created and updated. Generally, there is no review before modifications are accepted. Most edits to a wiki page can be made in real-time, and appear almost instantaneously online. This can often lead to abuse of the system.

One primary problem with wiki's is that some pedophiles have been known to modify various terms on sites like wikipedia.com, in an attempt to shine a more positive light on themselves, and the acts they perform.

Usenet Newsgroups

Usenet is one of the oldest computer network communications systems still in widespread use. It was established in 1980 following experiments the previous year, over a decade before the World Wide Web was introduced and the general public was admitted access to the Internet. It was originally conceived as a method to post research news and announcements.

Today, almost all Usenet traffic is carried over the Internet. The current format and transmission of Usenet articles is very similar to that of Internet email messages. However, whereas email is usually used for one-to-one communication, Usenet allow distribution of information to millions of users.

The articles that users post to Usenet are organized into topical categories called newsgroups, which are themselves logically organized into hierarchies of subjects. For instance, "sci.math" and "sci.physics" are within the "sci" hierarchy, for science. When a user subscribes to a newsgroup, the news client software keeps track of which articles that user has read.

Usenet is of significant cultural importance in the networked world, having given rise to, or popularized, many widely recognized concepts and terms such as "FAQ" and "spam".

Today, Usenet has diminished in importance with respect to mailing lists and weblogs. The difference from mailing lists though, is that Usenet requires no personal registration with the group concerned. The archives are always available, and reading the Usenet messages requires no mail client, but it does require a news client which is included in most modern e-mail clients.

Usenet Newsgroups are typically accessed with special client software that connects to a news server. With the rise of the World Wide Web, web front-ends have sometimes been used to access newsgroups via news-to-web gateways. However, these gateways often provide limited features, and for that reason using a local client is still regarded as the best way to access newsgroups.

Newsreader clients are available for all major operating systems and come in all shapes and sizes. Many eMail clients also have an integrated newsreader, such as Microsoft's Outlook Express.

A minority of newsgroups are moderated. That means that messages submitted by readers are not distributed to the public until the moderator of the newsgroup approves the posting. Moderated newsgroups have rules called charters. Moderators are persons whose job is to ensure that messages that the readers see in newsgroups conform to the charter of the newsgroup. Typically, moderators are appointed in the proposal for the newsgroup, and changes of moderators follow a succession plan.

The job of the moderator is to receive submitted articles, review them, and release only approved articles so that they can be properly propagated worldwide. Such articles must will contain an header line titled "Approved" and may contain the email address of the moderator that approved the article for distribution.

Unmoderated newsgroups form the majority of Usenet newsgroups, and messages submitted by readers for unmoderated newsgroups are immediately propagated world wide for everyone to see.

Organization of Usenet Groups

The major set of Usenet Newsgroups is contained within eight hierarchies, operated under consensual guidelines that govern their administration and naming. The current "Big Eight" are:

- comp.*: computer-related discussions (comp.software, comp.sys.amiga)
- misc.*: Miscellaneous topics (misc.education, misc.forsale, misc.kids)

- news.*: Discussions and announcements about news (meaning Usenet, not current events) (news.groups, news.admin)
- rec.*: Recreation and entertainment (rec.music, rec.arts.movies)
- sci.*: Science related discussions (sci.psychology, sci.research)
- soc.*: Social discussions (soc.college.org, soc.culture.african)
- talk.*: Talk about various controversial topics (talk.religion, talk.politics)
- humanities.*: Fine arts, literature, and philosophy (humanities.classics, humanities.design.misc)

(Note: the asterisks are used as wildcard patterns, examples follow in parentheses)

The "alt.*" hierarchy is not subject to the procedures controlling groups in the Big Eight, and it is as a result less organized and much more dangerous. Groups in the "alt.*" hierarchy tend to be more specialized. For example, there might be a newsgroup under the Big Eight which contains discussions about children's books, but a group in the "alt" hierarchy may be dedicated to one specific author of children's books.

Another sub-group of the "alt" group is alt.binaries.*, making it the largest of all the hierarchies. These sub-groups contain digital pictures or software.

Many other hierarchies of newsgroups are distributed alongside these. Regional and language-specific hierarchies such as "japan.*" and "nl.*" serve specific regions such as Japan and the Netherlands. Companies such as Microsoft administer their own hierarchies to discuss their products and offer community technical support.

The "alt.*" groups have generally been created by less than reputable people. That's not to say that every group in the "alt.*" newsgroup is bad, but a rather large group of criminals from all walks of life, from pedophiles to credit card thieves, computer hackers to check forgers use the "alt.*" groups to exchange information.

Here is a small sample of some of the "alt.*" newsgroups and the type of information found in these groups:

- **Alt.2600**: Used by phone phreaks to exchange information about stealing telephone services from the phone company.

- **Alt.aol.phishing**: Users of this group exchange information on AOL users, and discuss methods for obtaining personal information about AOL users.

- **Alt.drugdealers**: Users of this group exchange information on locating drug dealers, and drug dealers use this group to increase business. Information in these groups is generally coded in such a way that only those who are "In the Know" will under stand the messages.

- **Alt.drug.testing**: Users of this group exchange information relating to beating drug tests.

- **Alt.art.theft**: These users discuss stolen art, and methods to perpetrate those crimes. This site may look nefarious at first, but this site actually discusses past thefts.

- **Alt.fraud**: These users exchange information on fraud scams, and discuss how to improve on fraud scams, and develop new fraud scams.

- **Alt.hipcrime.collecting.credit-cards.numbers**: This group is often used to exchange credit card information that has been stolen from various sources.

- **Alt.binaries.pedophile**: Pedophiles use this group to exchange photos of children, and exchange methods used to access children, including kidnapping.

Gnutella

Gnutella, pronounced with a silent "g" as "nutella", is a file sharing network protocol used primarily to exchange files, and was originally created to share music files. However, due to its popularity and decentralized structure; people started sharing other files, such as software, documents, books and pornography.

As a decentralized network it is impossible for authorities to shutdown the network, and it becomes impossible to monitor and control the content being exchanged. Bearshare, Frostwire, Gnucleus, Limewire, Morpheus, Mutella, and XoloX are some of the most popular Gnutella clients.

Some Gnutella clients offer parental controls so that parents can restrict access to some types of files, such as adult content. However, most clients do not offer much in the area of security for parental controls, and knowledgeable teens can easily bypass these security features.

The largest problem with the network of Gnutella clients is that it is completely decentralized, and nearly impossible to police. Content can easily be distributed to millions of people, with no verification of age, and in a nearly anonymous environment. As a result of this lack of access logs, and no need to establish an account, pedophiles have quickly adopted the use of Gnutella networks to exchange illegal photos, and other information.

How Gnutella works

To envision how Gnutella works, imagine a large circle of users, called nodes, each node is running Gnutella client software. On initial startup, the client software will search to find at least one other node. Once connected, the client will request a list of working addresses. The client will then try to connect to the nodes stored in its own database, as well as nodes it receives from other clients until it reaches a certain quota.

Now, when the user wants to do a search, the client will send the request to each node it is actively connected to. The number of actively connected nodes for a client is usually quite small, around 5, so each node then forwards the request to all the nodes it is connected to, and they in turn forward the request, and so on, until the packet has completed a predetermined number of jumps or hops from the sender.

If a search request turns up a result, the node that had the result needs to contact the searcher. It sends a response message back along the route the query came through, as the query itself did not contain identifying information of the original node.

When the user disconnects, the Gnutella client software saves the list of nodes that it was actively connected to, or was keeping as a backup, for use the next time it attempts to connect.

Gnutella Security Issues

Security on the Gnutella network is up to the individual user loading a Gnutella client, and can create one of the largest security holes in your network.

When you install a Gnutella client, most are preconfigured to allow searching of your computer as part of the Gnutella network. In most cases this is limited to a select list of directories, usually part of the Gnutella client itself. However, some clients may scan your entire disk drive and make all your computer files searchable by the entire world, circumventing any firewalls, antivirus software and any other security features you have established.

There have been cases of identity theft as a result of someone performing a simple Gnutella search for any file with a ".doc" or ".txt" or ".tax" extension. Then simply downloading the files returned in the search.

In one such case a woman's previous taxes where downloaded, containing address, social security numbers for all family members, annual income, employers, copies of W2's, and anything, and everything need to steal her identity.

Additionally, since individual Gnutella node users, determine what is made available for the world to see, there are some people that will name a file using a simple, harmless file name, but such as "sunrise.jpg", that is actually an adult photo, or they may name a file using the name of a new song as an "mp3" file, but when it is actually played, it's a personal recording that you would not want your children to listen to.

Bottom line, you can not trust any content downloaded over a Gnutella network or the Internet for that matter. What may look harmless could be illegal pictures, bootleg software, illegal music, or someone's personal information. Gnutella networks should be avoided at all costs.

Another issue with Gnutella is its perceived anonymity. On the internet, there is no such thing as anonymity. Every computer connected to the internet has an IP address, which both your Internet Service provider logs and the Gnutella client will use to connect to your computer. These IP addresses can easily be traced in a matter of seconds anywhere in the world.

In recent months the, Recording Institute Association of America, or RIAA has successfully sued many Gnutella users for distributing copyrighted music over the internet using Gnutella clients.

The RIAA uses custom Gnutella software to search for Gnutella clients that are distributing copyrighted music. They are then able to request a copy of the file, which results in an exchange of IP addresses of the Gnutella clients.

Once they have the IP address of the Gnutella client, in hand, they can easily locate the ISP (Internet Service Provider), which owns the IP address. They can then request the name and address of the ISP's customer that was using the assigned IP at the time of the download. Once they have that information, they can easily file charges for copyright infringement.

Home Networking

In this section I will discuss several items commonly found in home networks. You may be familiar with some of the terms, and others may be new to you, but all are commonly found in home networks.

Modems

A modem is a device that modulates a carrier signal to encode digital information, and also demodulates such a carrier signal to decode the transmitted information. The goal is to produce a signal that can be transmitted easily and decoded to reproduce the original digital data.

The most familiar example of a modem turns the digital '1s and 0s' of a personal computer into sounds that can be transmitted over the telephone lines of Plain Old Telephone System (POTS), and once received on the other side, converts those sounds back into 1s and 0s. Modems are generally classified by the amount of data they can send in a given time, normally measured in bits per second, or "bps".

Routers

A router acts as a junction between two or more networks to transfer data packets among them. A router is different from a switch that connects devices to form a Local Area Network (LAN). One easy illustration for the different functions of routers and switches is to think of switches as neighborhood streets, and the router as the intersections with the street signs. Each house on the street has an address within a range on the block. In the same way, a switch connects various devices each with their own IP address(es) on a LAN. However, the switch knows nothing about IP addresses except its own management address. Routers connect networks together the way that on-ramps or major intersections connect streets to both highways and freeways, etc. The street signs at the intersection (routing table) show which way the packets need to flow.

For example, a router at home connects the Internet Service Provider's (ISP) network (usually on an Internet address) together with the LAN in the home (typically using a range of private IP addresses) and a single broadcast domain. The switch connects devices together to form the LAN. Sometimes the switch and the router are combined together in one single package sold as a multiple port router.

In order to route packets, a router communicates with other routers using routing protocols and using this information creates and maintains a routing table. The routing table stores the best routes to certain network destinations, and the path to the next router.

Wireless LAN

A wireless LAN or WLAN is a wireless local area network, which is the linking of two or more computers with-out using wires. It is the same as a LAN, but has a wireless interface. WLAN utilizes spread-spectrum technology based on radio waves to enable communication between devices in a limited area, also known as the basic service set. This gives users the mobility to move around within a broad coverage area and still be connected to the network.

Hubs & Switches

A hub is a fairly unsophisticated broadcast device. Any packet entering any port is broadcast out on every port and thus hubs do not manage any of the traffic that comes through their ports. Since every packet is constantly being sent out through every port, you end up with packet collisions, which greatly impede the smooth flow of traffic on your local area network or LAN.

A switch, on the other hand, isolates ports which means every received packet is sent out only to the port on which the target may be found however, if the proper port cannot be determined, then the switch will broadcast the packet to all ports. Since the switch intelligently sends packets only where they need to go, and not everywhere, the performance speed of your network can be greatly increased.

Firewall

A firewall is a device which functions in a networked environment to prevent some communications forbidden by a security policy.

A firewall can be either a hardware device than connect between your local network and the internet. A firewall can also be software based and can run on your local PC, such as Microsoft's firewall found in Windows XP.

A firewall has the basic task of controlling traffic between different zones of trust. Typical zones of trust include the Internet (a zone with no trust) and an internal network (a zone with high trust) such as your home network. The ultimate goal is to provide controlled connectivity between zones of differing trust levels through the enforcement of a security policy and connectivity model based on the least privilege principle.

Proper configuration of firewalls demands skill from the administrator. It requires considerable understanding of network protocols and of computer security. Small mistakes can render a firewall worthless as a security tool.

Proxy Servers

A proxy server is a computer that offer a filtered path to another network such as the internet. Client computers on a private network will send their requests for web pages, email and any other services via the proxy server computer.

Proxy servers can also filter the content of Web pages served which attempt to block offensive Web content. In some cases virus protection can also be incorporated into a proxy server which will filter out many viruses before they get you the user's computer. In this fashion, a single computer can handle filtering for many computers on a single network.

Recommendations

Most people do not need the level of security for their networks that the military uses, but no protection is not an option these days. It should also be noted that there is no way to completely protect your computer, other that turning it off, and leaving it off.

Listed here are a few suggestions that can make your internet experience safe and secure, and reduce your level of vulnerability on the internet.

Consult your Employer

If you use your broadband access to connect to your employer's network via a Virtual Private Network (VPN) or other means, your employer may have policies or procedures relating to the security of your home network. Be sure to consult with your employer's support personnel, as appropriate, to ensure that your company's network is secure as well.

Use virus protection software

It is recommended that you use anti-virus software on all Internet-connected computers that will access the internet. Be sure to keep your anti-virus software up-to-date. Many anti-virus packages support automatic updates of virus definitions. I recommend the use of these automatic updates when available.

Use a firewall

It is strongly recommend that you use some type of firewall product, such as a network appliance or a personal firewall software package. Intruders are constantly scanning home user systems for known vulnerabilities. Network firewalls, whether software or hardware-based, can provide some degree of protection against these attacks. However, no firewall can detect or stop all attacks, so it's not sufficient to install a firewall and then ignore all other security measures.

Use Content Filtering Software

If you have children, it is strongly recommended that you use content filtering software, or parental control software. Most of the software available for content filtering can offer significant levels of protection for your children.

Research the available parental control software, and select the software that meets your requirements, and enforces your family standards.

See Parental Control Software, under Software Tools later in this book for a list of available software applications.

Secure your wireless LAN

Wireless networks do not end at your walls, ceiling, or floor. Wireless routers or access points use high frequency radio wave, and travel as far as 100 feet or more in some cases.

This allows anyone in range of your wireless router to gain access to your wireless home network. This means that any of your neighbors could easily tap into, and use your broadband connect to send email, visit illegal porn sites, download software, or music, which will all be logged in the internet to the IP Address assigned to you by your ISP.

To prevent this abuse of your network, it is highly recommended that you read the instruction that accompanied your wireless router or access point, and secure it.

Most wireless LAN or WLAN hardware has gotten easy enough to set up that many users simply plug it in and start using the network without giving much thought to security. Nevertheless, taking a few extra minutes to configure the security features of your wireless router or access point is time well spent.

Here are some of the things you can do to protect your wireless network:

- Secure your wireless router or access point administration interface by assigning a password at the time you configure your router. By not securing your wireless router, anyone within range can easily take control of your network, and use your Internet connection to download or upload illegal photos, pirate software, or send threatening emails.

- Don't broadcast your Service Set Identifier or SSID. Broadcasting your SSID is like placing a billboard on your front lawn that says, "Free Internet Access Here!". Anyone within range of your wireless router will automatically see you network.

- Enable WPA encryption instead of WEP. WPA encryption is a much more secure communication method, and was designed to address several serious security concerns that effect WEP. There are software systems designed to crack WEP security, which would allow other to use your network for their own illegal purposes.

- Use MAC filtering for access control. Every network device has a MAC or Media Access Control ID. By entering the MAC for each computer on your network, other will not be able to access your network unless their computers MAC has been added to the list of allowable computer.

- Disable remote administration. If remote administration is enable, then anyone on the Internet will have access to the login prompt for your router, and it won't take very long before someone is able to take control of your router, and use it to relay illegal messages or other content, through your Internet connection.

Do your neighbors have a wireless LAN

As previously stated above, your wireless transmissions do not stop at your walls. If you live in a condo, it is conceivable that all the apartments adjacent to yours, can access your wireless LAN.

The same holds true for you. If someone in close proximity, such as an apartment in proximity to yours, has an unsecured wireless LAN, your children could access their network and have unrestricted access to the internet.

Even if you don't have a wireless LAN, that new laptop PC you purchased for your child may have a wireless Network Access card built in. This will allow your child to connect to any unsecured networks and have complete freedom on the net.

Check with your neighbors and see if they have a wireless LAN. If they do, make sure they have access security configured on their wireless router. Explain your concerns about your child, and the potential for others to access the wireless network. Hopefully, they will understand, and take the required steps to secure their network.

Make sure your child's computer has adequate parental control software installed on the computer they will be using. This will offer some protection.

Don't open unknown email attachments

Before opening any email attachments, be sure you know the source of the attachment. It is not enough that the mail originated from an address you recognize. The Melissa virus spread precisely because it originated from a familiar address. Malicious code might be distributed in amusing or enticing programs.

If you must open an attachment before you can verify the source, I suggest the following procedure:

- be sure your virus definitions are up-to-date
- save the file to your hard disk
- scan the file using your antivirus software

For additional protection, you can disconnect your computer's network connection before opening the file. This will prevent any virus' that access the internet.

Following these steps will reduce, but not wholly eliminate, the chance that any malicious code contained in the attachment might spread from your computer to others.

Don't run programs of unknown origin

Never run a program unless you know it to be authored by a person or company that you trust. Also, don't send programs of unknown origin to your friends or coworkers simply because they are amusing, they might contain a virus or other harmful program.

Disable hidden filename extensions

Windows operating systems contain an option to "Hide file extensions for known file types". The option is enabled by default, but you can disable this option in order to have file extensions displayed by Windows. After disabling this option, there are still some file extensions that, by default, will continue to remain hidden.

There is a registry value which, if set, will cause Windows to hide certain file extensions regardless of user configuration choices elsewhere in the operating system. The "NeverShowExt" registry value is used to hide the extensions for basic Windows file types. For example, the ".LNK" extension associated with Windows shortcuts remains hidden even after a user has turned off the option to hide extensions.

Virus writer have been known to exploit hidden file extension by renaming a virus program with an ".exe" extension so that it appears to be a picture with an extension ".gif".

For example, is a person had a virus program named "virus.exe" most people would understand it is a virus and would not attempt to open the file. However, if the program where named, "Mypicture.exe" some people may notice it, but the ".exe" extension indicates this file is a program and not a photo. If extensions are hidden, Most people would see the file and as "Mypicture".

Virus writes will take this one step further by adding a second extension, and rename the file as "Mypicture.gif.exe". On a system with hidden extensions, this file would appears as "Mypicture.gif" and could easily be mistaken as a photo. An unwitting person may attempt to open this "Picture" and end up running the virus.

By making sure all extensions are visible, you can easily identify some potential viruses

Keep your operating system patched

Most software vender will occasionally make changes to their software. They may discover security vulnerabilities, or other programming issues that hackers, or virus' can exploit. To "Patch" these security holes, vendors such as Microsoft, release what are called patches.

Microsoft Windows has a rather extensive automatic patch update capability. As well as some applications will automatically check for available updates, and many vendors offer automatic notification of updates via a mailing list. Look on your vendor's web site for information about automatic notification. If no mailing list or other automated notification mechanism is offered you may need to check periodically for updates.

Turn off your Computer

Turn off your computer or disconnect its Ethernet interface when you are not using it. An intruder cannot attack your computer if it is powered off or otherwise completely disconnected from the network.

Disable Java, JavaScript, and ActiveX if possible

Be aware of the risks involved in the use of "mobile code" such as ActiveX, Java, and JavaScript. A malicious web developer may attach a script to something sent to a web site, such as a URL, an element in a form, or a database inquiry. Later, when the web site responds to you, the malicious script is transferred to your browser.

The most significant impact of this vulnerability can be avoided by disabling all scripting languages. Turning off these options will keep you from being vulnerable to malicious scripts. However, it will limit the interaction you can have with some web sites.

Many legitimate sites use scripts running within the browser to add useful features. Disabling scripting may degrade the functionality of these sites.

Disable scripting features in email programs

Because many email programs use the same code as web browsers to display HTML, vulnerabilities that affect ActiveX, Java, and JavaScript are often applicable to email as well as web pages. Therefore, in addition to disabling scripting features in web browsers, it is also recommend that users also disable these features in their email programs.

Make regular backups of critical data

Keep a copy of important files on removable media such as ZIP disks or recordable CD-ROM, or DVD-ROM disks. Use software backup tools if available, and store the backup disks somewhere away from the computer, ideally in a water-proof, and fire resistant safe. It is also recommended that you create a copy of your backup and keep that copy outside of your house, perhaps a safe deposit box. That way your critical information is safe in the event of some other disaster.

Make a boot disk

To aid in recovering from a security breach or hard disk failure, create a boot disk on a floppy disk which will help when recovering a computer after such an event has occurred. Remember, however, you must create this disk before you have a security event.

Reference your system documentation to learn how to create a boot floppy on your specific system.

Online Predators

One of the attractions of the Internet is the anonymity of the user, and this is why it can be so dangerous. A child doesn't always know with whom he or she is interacting. Children may think they know, but unless it's a school friend or a relative, they really can't be sure. Often we think of pedophiles as having access to children out on the playground and other places, but because of the way the Internet works; children can actually be interacting on their home computers with adults who pretend to be a child of the same age.

Child sexual exploitation occurs in every economic, social, ethnic, and religious group. With the Internet becoming a more powerful, worldwide medium, the danger to children has drastically increased. Pedophiles and other sexual predators use the Internet to exchange names and addresses of other predators and potential child victims. Using screen names as aliases, they gather online and swap child pornography with amazing speed and in quantities beyond our wildest imaginations.

Never before have predators, had the opportunity to communicate so freely and directly with each other as they do online. Their communication on the Internet provides validation, or virtual validation, for their behavior. Predators share their conquests, real and imagined. They discuss ways to contact and lure children online and exchange tips on seduction techniques. Predators are using the technology of the Internet to train and encourage each other to act out sexually with children.

The Internet also serves as a tool for predators to exchange tips on the avoidance of law enforcement detection. Tech savvy Predators can find countless methods to avoid having phone calls recorded, or traced. They can learn how to make internet IP tracking more difficult, and how to create computer viruses to help them gain access to your child.

Children, especially adolescents, are sometimes interested in and curious about sexuality and sexually explicit material. They may be moving away from the total control of parents and seeking to establish new relationships outside their family. Because they may be curious, children/adolescents sometimes use their on-line access to actively seek out such materials and individuals. Sex offenders targeting children will use and exploit these characteristics and needs. Some children may also be attracted to and lured by on-line offenders closer to their age who, although not technically child molesters, may be dangerous. Nevertheless, they have been seduced and manipulated by a clever offender and do not fully understand or recognize the potential danger of these contacts.

Know the Risks - Online Predators

Using Internet communication tools such as chat rooms, e-mail and instant messaging can put children and teens at risk of encountering online predators. The assumed anonymity of the Internet means that trust and intimacy can develop quickly online. Predators take advantage of this anonymity to build online relationships with inexperienced young people.

Adults can help protect children by becoming aware of the risks related to online communication and being involved in their children's Internet activities.

How do online predators operate?

Predators establish contact with children through conversations in chat rooms, instant messaging, and e-mail or discussion boards. They often misrepresent their age and pretend to be younger, usually closer in age to their victim. Many children use 'peer support' online forums to deal with their problems and predators often go to these areas to look for vulnerable victims.

Online predators try to gradually seduce their targets through attention, affection, kindness, and even gifts, and often devote considerable time, money and energy to this effort. They are aware of the latest music and hobbies likely to interest children. They listen to and sympathize with children's problems. They have learned how to write e-mail and text messages using the lingo used by children so they do not look out of place.

They also try to ease children's inhibitions by gradually introducing sexual content into their conversations or by showing them sexually explicit material.

Some predators work faster than others, engaging in sexually explicit conversations immediately. This more direct approach may include harassment or stalking. Predators may also evaluate the children they meet online for future face-to-face contact.

Which children people are at risk?

Children aged 10 to 17 are the most vulnerable age group and are at high risk of being approached by online predators. They are exploring their sexuality, moving away from parental control and looking for new relationships outside the family. Under the guise of anonymity, they are more likely to take risks online without fully understanding the possible implications.

Children who are most vulnerable to online predators tend to be:

- new to online activity and unfamiliar with Internet etiquette or "Netiquette"
- actively seeking attention or affection
- rebellious
- isolated or lonely

- curious
- confused regarding sexual identity
- easily tricked by adults
- susceptible to peer pressure
- attracted by subcultures apart from their parents' world

Kids feel they are aware of the dangers of predators, but in reality they are quite naive about online relationships. In focus groups conducted by the Media Awareness Network in 2000, girls aged 11 to 14 initially said they disguised their identities in chat rooms. They admitted, however, that it was impossible to maintain a false identity for long and eventually revealed personal information when they felt they could 'trust a person.' Building this 'trust' took from 15 minutes to several weeks – not a long time for a skilful predator to wait.

What Are Signs That Your Child Might Be At Risk On-line?

If your child spends large amounts of time on-line, especially at night.

Most children that fall victim to computer-sex offenders spend large amounts of time on-line, particularly in chat rooms. They may go on-line after dinner and on the weekends. They may be latchkey kids whose parents have told them to stay at home after school. They go on-line to chat with friends, make new friends, pass time, and sometimes look for sexually explicit information. While much of the knowledge and experience gained on the computer may be valuable, parents should consider monitoring the amount of time spent on-line.

Children on-line are at the greatest risk during the evening hours. While offenders are on-line around the clock, most work during the day and spend their evenings on-line trying to locate and lure children or seek pornography.

If you find pornography on your child's computer.

Pornography is often used in the sexual victimization of children. Sex offenders often supply their potential victims with pornography as a means of opening sexual discussions and for seduction. Child pornography may be used to show the child victim that sex between children and adults is "normal." Parents should be conscious of the fact that a child may hide the pornographic files from their parents by placing it on diskettes.

If your child receives phone calls from someone you don't know or makes calls, sometimes long distance, to numbers you don't recognize.

While talking to a child victim on-line is a thrill for a computer-sex offender, it can be very cumbersome. Most want to talk to the children on the telephone. They often engage in "phone sex" with the children and often seek to set up an actual meeting for real sex.

While a child may be hesitant to give out his/her home phone number, the computer-sex offenders will give out theirs. With Caller ID, they can readily find out the child's phone number. Some computer-sex offenders have even obtained toll-free 800 numbers, so that their potential victims can call them without their parents finding out. Others will tell the child to call collect. Both of these methods result in the computer-sex offender being able to find out the child's phone number.

If your child receives mail, gifts, or packages from someone you don't know.

As part of the seduction process, it is common for offenders to send letters, photographs, and all manner of gifts to their potential victims. Computer-sex offenders have even sent plane tickets in order for the child to travel across the country to meet them.

If your child turns the computer monitor off or quickly changes the screen on the monitor when you come into the room.

A child looking at pornographic images or having sexually explicit conversations does not want you to see it on the screen. They will often quickly turn the monitor off, or change screens to prevent your from seeing what they are doing on the computer.

If your child becomes withdrawn from the family.

Computer-sex offenders will work very hard at driving a wedge between a child and their family or at exploiting their relationship. They will accentuate any minor problems at home that the child might have.

Parents should be alert to potential indicators of sexual exploitation:

- changes in behavior, extreme mood swings, withdrawal, fearfulness, and excessive crying
- bed-wetting, nightmares, fear of going to bed, or other sleep disturbances
- acting out inappropriate sexual activity or showing an unusual interest in sexual matters
- a sudden acting out of feelings or aggressive or rebellious behavior
- regression to infantile behavior
- a fear of certain places, people, or activities, especially being alone with certain people because children of any age should not be forced to give affection to anyone if they don't want to
- be alert to signs that your children are trying to avoid someone, and listen care-

fully when your children tell you how they feel about someone

- pain, itching, bleeding, fluid, or rawness in the private areas

If you observe any of these behaviors in your children, talk to them about the causes. Behavioral changes such as these may be due to causes other than sexual exploitation such as a medical, family, or school problem, but be sure to work with your child to get to the root of the problem. Also keep in mind that sometimes children do not always demonstrate obvious signs such as these but may do or say something that hints at the exploitation.

If your child is using an on-line account belonging to someone else.

Even if you don't subscribe to an on-line service or Internet service, your child may meet an offender while on-line at a friend's house or the library. Most computers come preloaded with on-line and/or Internet software. Computer-sex offenders will sometimes provide potential victims with a computer account for communications with them.

What Should You Do If You Suspect Your Child Is Communicating With A Sexual Predator On-line?

- Review what is on your child's computer. If you don't know how, ask a friend, coworker, relative, or other knowledgeable person. Pornography or any kind of sexual communication can be a warning sign.

- Talk openly with your child about your suspicions. Tell them about the dangers of computer-sex offenders.

- Use the Caller ID service to determine who is calling your child. Most telephone companies that offer Caller ID also offer a service that allows you to block your number from appearing on someone else's Caller ID. Telephone companies also offer an additional service feature that rejects incoming calls that you block. This rejection feature prevents computer-sex offenders or anyone else from calling your home anonymously.

- Devices can be purchased that show telephone numbers that have been dialed from your home phone. If you don't have one of these devices. But you have access to a numeric pager, the last number called from your home phone can be retrieved provided that the telephone is equipped with a redial feature.

This is done using a numeric-display pager and another phone that is on the same line as the first phone with the redial feature. Using the two phones and the pager, a call is placed from the second phone to the pager. When the paging terminal beeps for you to enter a telephone number, you press the redial button on the first (or suspect) phone. The last number called from that phone will then be displayed on the pager.

- Monitor your child's access to all types of live electronic communications (i.e., chat rooms, instant messages, Internet Relay Chat, etc.), and monitor your child's e-mail. Computer-sex offenders almost always meet potential victims via chat rooms. After meeting a child on-line, they will continue to communicate electronically often via e-mail.

What Should You Do If You Find Your Child Is Communicating With A Sexual Predator On-line?

Should any of the following situations arise in your household, via the Internet or on-line service, you should immediately contact your local or state law enforcement agency, the FBI, and the National Center for Missing and Exploited Children:

1. Your child or anyone in the household has received child pornography;
2. Your child has been sexually solicited by someone who knows that your child is under 18 years of age;
3. Your child has received sexually explicit images from someone that knows your child is under the age of 18.

If one of these scenarios occurs, keep the computer turned off in order to preserve any evidence for future law enforcement use. Unless directed to do so by the law enforcement agency, you should not attempt to copy any of the images and/or text found on the computer.

What Can You Do To Minimize The Chances Of An On-line Exploiter Victimizing Your Child?

- Keep the computer in a common room in the house, do not keep it in your child's bedroom. It is much more difficult for a computer-sex offender to communicate with a child when the computer screen is visible to a parent or another member of the household.

- Communicate, and talk to your child about sexual victimization and potential on-line danger.

- Spend time with your children on-line. Have them teach you about their favorite on-line destinations.

- Utilize parental controls provided by your service provider and/or blocking software. While electronic chat can be a great place for children to make new friends and discuss various topics of interest, it is also prowled by computer-sex offenders. Use of chat rooms, in particular, should be heavily monitored. While parents should utilize these mechanisms, they should not totally rely on them.

- Always maintain access to your child's on-line account and randomly check his/her e-mail. Be aware that your child could be contacted through the U.S. Mail. Some predators may send gifts such as web camera, or sexually explicit material. Be up front with your child about your access and reasons why.

- Teach your child how to use on-line resources responsibly. There is much more to the on-line experience than chat rooms.

- Find out what computer safeguards are utilized by your child's school, the public library, and at the homes of your child's friends. These are all places, outside your normal supervision, where your child could encounter an on-line predator.

- Understand, even if your child was a willing participant in any form of sexual exploitation, that he/she is not at fault and is the victim. The offender always bears the complete responsibility for his or her actions.

- Instruct your children:

    o to never arrange a face-to-face meeting with someone they met on- line
    o to never upload (post) pictures of themselves onto the Internet or on-line service to people they do not personally know
    o to never give out identifying information such as their name, home address, school name, or telephone number
    o to never download pictures from an unknown source, as there is a good chance there could be sexually explicit images

- o to never respond to messages or bulletin board postings that are suggestive, obscene, belligerent, or harassing
- o that whatever they are told on-line may or may not be true.

Children as Victims on the Internet

While I research this book, I read countless FBI reports on the subject of child exploitation, and predators. I was alarmed by the various types of pornography that are being generated on-line.

The amount and content of depraved material available on the Internet to any child who stumbles across it, is truly saddening. The common practice of today's Internet "porno-preneur" is the posting of free teaser images on their web sites as enticements to solicit new subscribers. Any child with unrestricted Internet access can view these free pictures through accidentally accessing such sites or by deliberately searching them out. Any computer-literate child can view adult pornography, such as images that appear in Playboy or Penthouse, as well as pornography that is prosecutable as obscenity, which might include pictures of bestiality, child pornography; and the rape, torture, and mutilation of women.

Pornographic Web Sites

It used to be that the only place porn was available was at the local convenient store, and you had to have valid identification proving that you were over 18 years of age.

Today nearly anyone can obtain all the porn they want on the internet, from simple nudity to the highest degree of illegal porn. The internet has revolutionized the demoralization of society. Money hungry pornographers that are only interested in cash flow, and could care less about who is viewing the content they publish has given the Internet a bad reputation.

Pornographic images are not the only harmful images on the Internet. There are also war photos, video of actual rapes, and crime scene photos that can all cause considerable harm to young children.

Hate on the Web

The Internet has created a medium for white supremacist groups, the neo-Nazis, the Skinheads, the Ku Klux Klan, and the Aryan Nations to publish their message, and spread it to the masses. These organizations use the Internet to spread their message, collect intelligence on people and organization, and distribute objectives, orders, and plans to further their cause. These organizations are concerned with who is reading their propaganda. They want your children to see it! They want your children! They want your children to spread their message to as many of their school friends as they can.

Anyone with access to a search engine, such as Google, Lycos or Yahoo can easily locate these sites, whether intentionally or unintentionally.

Anarchists on the Web

Anarchist also spread their word on the Internet, speaking out against the government and any other rules based establishment.

Every parent wants their children to learn, to expand their knowledge, and hopefully change the world for the better. Unfortunately, some children learn about anarchists and become tainted by the message.

A perfect example of this happened on April 20, 1999 at Columbine High School, when two teenage students, Eric Harris and Dylan Klebold, carried out a shooting rampage, killing 12 fellow students and a teacher, as well as wounding 24 others, before committing suicide. It is considered to be the deadliest school shooting in United States History.

Upon searching the homes of Eric Harris and Dylan Klebold, the FBI found extensive instructions obtained from the Internet. Documents such as "The Anarchist Cookbook" provided detailed instructions on bomb building. Instructions they used to build 99 improvised explosive devices of various designs and sizes.

How children access this information

As children get older they become curious, and the Internet allows them to research those things that they are curious about. Unfortunately, they may seek out information about anarchist, racism, and any number of subjects they may not be ready to fully comprehend. This is when it becomes the most harmful, because they are willfully seeking out the information and may be receptive to the information and views they find on-line.

Unintentional Access

You're a careful parent and have taken every precaution. You have taught your children never to open email from spammers, or meet with strangers met in chat rooms, and they have followed the rules and have become wise internet surfers. But children do not have the wisdom that adults have, and at times may fall for a spam email or click on an innocent looking link.

No matter how honest your child is, and no matter how well you have taught them, they may be duped into inadvertently visiting an adult website.

Unfortunately, many industries use less than credible methods for advertisement. These companies are not limited to pornography, or get rich quick scams. Drug distributors, health care products, diet supplements along with many others have used these types of practices.

Innocent, imprecise, misdirected searches

As with email attachments and viruses previously mentioned, companies will attempt to increase website traffic to their sites by using popular search terms.

When a Website author creates a web page, they will generally program a list of related search terms for the site.

These terms are referred to as Meta Variables, and are used by search engines to index a website. For example, a website for sports may have a list of Meta Variables such as, "sports", "football", "baseball", "basketball", "racing" and so on. By adding these Meta Variables to a site, a person performing a web search may enter "Sports" or "football" and the search engine will display the sites that contain these search terms in their Meta list.

Porn site promoters, trying to increase web site traffic will add commonly used search words and terms in their Meta Variable list. For example, a porn site may use the Meta Variables, "sports", "school", "whitehouse", "congress", "photography", "Britney Spears" or any number of terms people use to search the web. As a result, when children key in their favorite search terms, pornographic sites pop up along with the sites the children are seeking.

Unfortunately, unless you are using filtering software, most search engines don't distinguish between an adult's search request and a child's.

Stealth sites and misleading URLs

Pornographers are businesses that rely on increased site traffic. To build that traffic, one method they rely on is typographical errors when trying to visit a web site.

To help increase site traffic, pornographers purchase domain names such as the .com equivalent of a popular ".gov" or ".org" website, knowing full well that web surfers are likely to end up on their pornographic site instead of their desired destination.

Many children seeking information on the nation's Whitehouse may find themselves on a porn site instead of the official site at www.whitehouse.gov simply because they typed ".com" rather than ".gov".

Businesses and the Federal Government have actively pursued copyright, and trademark infringement charges against many of these websites. The pornographic website at www.whitehouse.com has been shutdown because of complaints by parents. However, there are still many adult web sites that rely on miss typed URL's to increase traffic.

The misuse of brand names

According to a recent study in England, 26 popular children's characters, such as Pokemon, My Little Pony and Action Man, revealed thousands of links to porn sites when entered into any of the popular search engines. 30 percent of the sites were hard-core pornography. 25 percent of porn sites are estimated to misuse popular brand names in search engine magnets, meta-tags and links. Three of the top ten brand names used are; Disney, Barbie, and Nintendo, and are specifically design to lure children to their adult web sites.

The need to constantly say no

A friend of mine shared with me how his nine-year-old son (who couldn't care less about girls at his age) did a search for Beanie Babies. He found many links to Beanies, and "Hot

Cyber Babes!!" that appeared in the list. If he had clicked on that link, his son would have been connected to that site and would have been able to freely view pornographic pictures.

If he had viewed the free pictures, the site would have required a credit card number and a password. Without saying no at least three times, he would have seen the free pictures and the damage would have been done. The constant need to say no on these web sites, conflicts with a child's natural curiosity. If a child, out of curiosity or carelessness, clicks on such links, he or she may be exposed to material that can never be erased from their mind.

Unsolicited e-mail

Unsolicited commercial e-mail messages are referred to as spam. Spammers can get e-mail addresses in many ways and they send hundreds of thousands of pieces of junk e-mail every day. They try to boost traffic by advertising pornography for sale and "make-money-fast" schemes.

In the case of pornographic spam, children open their e-mail and find direct images from pornographic web sites. Many of these e-mails contain subject lines that are deceptive; for example, "Please Help Me!", "I have that Money I owe you!", "Hello from and friend!" or "RE: Your Request!" Who wouldn't open mail with those subject headings? Children and adults are unable to determine the mail's true contents until the mail is opened and read, and by that time its too late! The images have been seen and can not be forgotten. In addition, some Web browsers automatically open popup images to display images that may be pornographic. Also disturbing is the fact that a child can be automatically switched to adult Web page-exhibiting sexually explicit im-ages-without even clicking on the link!

There are also viruses that are designed to cause por-nographic popup windows to appear. There viruses are designed to increase traffic to a particular web site. With a click of the mouse on a seemingly harmless link, up pops a hard-core pornographic image, and an invitation to a Web site specializing in porn, or perhaps to a XXX-rated video. Imbed-ded in the email is a command that caused popup after popup of pornographic pictures. With each click on the Close Window button, causes a dozen more popup windows appear. The only thing that will stop the popup's is turning the com-puter off.

You may be asking why anyone would want to increase traffic this way. The answer is money! Pornographic web site owners will often sell advertising space on their sites. The rates for advertising on these sites, and most non-pornographic web sites, are based on the number of visitors or "Hits" a web site receives. So if the traffic increases, so do the advertising rates.

Web site owners will then use a part of the advertising proceed to pay various companies to increase traffic to their web sites, and will actually pay these companies a fee for each person that visits the web site. The payouts are small, usually ranging from 5 cent to 50 cents per new visitor, but they do add up.

In their effort to increase websites traffic, these companies don't want to rely on slow, expensive advertising, they want fast money. Their philosophy is why settle for 100 or 300 new visitors per month to a web site and only earn a few hundred dollars for their effort. So they develop virus software designed to spread to as many computers as possible, causing each computer to visit these websites resulting in hundreds of thousands, if not millions of new visitors per month, earning these companies millions.

These companies don't care who visits the web sites, they just want new visitors. Send e-mail to anyone they can, including your children.

Do you know your kids email address

Most kids these days have an email address. It may be and AOL screen name that you have assigned them for accessing AOL. The problem is, Mom and Dad can usually read that email, therefore, many kids, mostly teens, also have an email account on any number of web services such as, Hotmail, YahooMail, or GMail from Google. Some may even have and email account on all of these sites. Many web sites offer free email accounts to anyone that wants one. Children can easily visit any number of free email sites and obtain a private email address that you don't know about.

Most parents have no idea what their kids email address is, or what the password is for that matter. Make it a point to find! WebWatcher is capable of tracking where your children have email accounts, and what the login and password are.

Instant Messages (IM's)

"IM" is short for "instant messaging" and is a type of real time communication and is similar to a chat room. Both parties connect using specialize software that allows each party to type messages that are instantly received by the other party. Most Instant Messaging software allows each person to send pictures, video, and other data files to the other person.

Children are vulnerable to receiving pornographic content through private, real-time communication with sexual predators. In addition, when certain people think that their identities are somewhat anonymous and they have a captive audience, they tend to let down their guard, and will often give away far too much information about themselves.

Intentional Access

Even the most diligent parental guidance and supervision does not deter a child who is determined to view pornography on the Internet. Children have access to computers and the Internet not only at home, but in many other places-at school, libraries, or the home of a friend.

Though your child may not directly access pornography, he or she may come into contact with other children who are, since online pornography is widely available to the public at large. In the past, those who wanted to view hard-core pornography, particularly that which might be prosecutable, had to overcome the embarrassment of others watching them enter an adult bookstore or peep show. Obviously, it was very difficult for children to see hard-core pornography with these limitations. Even soft-core "men's" magazines are not sold to minors or displayed so minors can see them. The internet has changed all that, and pornography and other adult content is just a click away.

Web Cams

Web cams are video cameras that are connected to a PC, and make it possible to conduct video conferencing, record short video clips to send to someone, or take still photos.

The Internet has revolutionized communication on a global basis. Along with this revolution came the webcam. With sites like www.myspace.com and www.me.com children are publishing huge amounts of personal information about themselves. In most cases, the parents have no idea what information their children are making available to the world, until it's too late.

When it comes to webcam on your computer, the big question is why. There is little justification for allowing a child to have web cam access. They just don't need it! Many teens tend to lose many inhabitations while chatting on-line. Adding a web cam to the mix is asking for trouble!

An example of this happened late in 2005. A 13-year old boy named Justin had started using his webcam to make money. It started when someone he was chatting with, offered Justin $50 to sit in front of his computer with his shirt off, for 3 minutes. Justin figured, "Hey, I take my shirt off at the pool for nothing, why not get paid." Within a short time Justin had over 1,500 clients, and was earning hundreds of thousands of dollars, doing what ever his clients asked.

Justin is just one example of how technology is helping predators and pedophiles commit their crimes. Technology de-personalizes the interaction of people on-line. Many teens have no problem undressing in front of their computer; they don't make the connection that other people may be watching. Even if they are not currently chatting with someone on-line, and believe no one is watching, their acts in the bed room could easily be transmitted all over the world without their knowledge.

One girl found out the hard way, when she found a video clip of herself on the Internet, getting undressed to take a shower. What she did not realize was that a voyeur virus had made its way onto her computer. This voyeur virus was designed to infect a computer that and detect any web cam that may be attached. Once the virus locates a web cam, it then begins transmitting everything within site of the camera over the internet, where voyeurs sit and watch unsuspecting people all over the world go about their daily lives in front of their computers, unaware that their web cam is transmitting their every move to the world.

Your Child as a Perpetrator

Most parents can't imagine that their child could rob a bank, or commit credit card fraud. "Not my son!", or "My daughter would never do that!" They raised their children to be good and honest. Unfortunately, that is exactly what is happening on the Internet. Because of the perceived anonymity of the Internet, children are using the Internet to commit crimes they normally would never commit. Phishing, credit card fraud, piracy, scams, cyber terrorism, creation and distribution of viruses, spam and sexual harassment, and stalking! Many children that commit these crimes don't even know they are crimes. They get the idea from friends at school, or they read about it online, or from someone in a chat room.

Cyber harassment, stalking and threats

Peer pressure, jealousy, and social status have a huge effect on a child, especially a teen that is trying to fit in, or be accepted in some social click at school. Children as well as many adults have the misguided idea that you can send email, or post a message to a newsgroup, or say something in a chat room in complete anonymity. Well that couldn't be further from the truth! Teens are quick to gossip about someone in a chat room, or send email to their friends trashing someone's reputation. Email may be forwarded to other friends, and eventually social alliances change and email message that where kept from someone are suddenly being used against the person that originally sent them.

For example, teen boys often become infatuated with some girl they saw at school, and may become obsessed with her. Sending her email, or breaking into chat room conversations simply to speak to her. This behavior may continue even after she informs him she is not interested. At this point it becomes cyber stalking if he persists, or he may lash out and begin to harass her in an effort to punish her for rejecting him.

Credit Card Fraud

Many times teens will use their parents' credit card number to access pay-per view adult web sites. They figure since the amounts are small, usually between $9.00 and $20.00 per visit, their parents will never notice that small charge to the credit card, or will assume it was for something they forgot about.

Sometime they will use someone else's credit card, perhaps they found it on-line, or it was given to them by a friend who may have stolen it. Other times, teens will swap credit card numbers of their parents, thinking that it reduces the possibility of it being traced to them. They generally don't think they are committing a crime that could actually result in their arrest.

Some teens have also been known to use other people's credit cards to order computer hardware, and other expensive items on-line. They will then use an address of someone they know to be out of town. They will then watch for the delivery of the item to the specified address and then either intercept the package and sign for it, or if the package is left on the doorstep, which is the preferred method, they will simple take the package.

Free Porn Sites

One particular scam that is commonly distributed, and teens quickly fall victim, is Free Porn Sites. These sites distribute a special software package that they claim you need to access the site for free. The software requires you to use a conventional dial-up modem to access the site. The teens will follow the instructions, and quickly have access to a vast amount of porn, and bootleg software.

What they don't realize is that the "special software" is a telephone line hijacker. If you normally use a dial-up modem to access the internet, then this software will turn off the modems speaker, hang-up the phone to your ISP, and then dial a pay-per minute 900 number or some other number in a foreign country that will bill that phone $7.95 per minute or more.

Fraud and counterfeiting

Many kids have tried to scan and print money. They may be trying to us it in the school soda machine, or pass it off as real money at the local fast food chain. They quickly learn that the soda machine knows the difference, and the cashier knows what a real twenty dollar bill looks and feels like.

Other teens have been know to steal their parents checks or someone else's check, and either use the check to purchase a video game, computer hardware, or other item. The area of fraud, and specifically check fraud, which is a fast growing crime in this country, is a very extensive issue, and I would suggest my book, *"The Truth about Check Fraud"* to find out more about how some children commit check fraud.

Computer Intrusion

Most children who become involved in computer break-ins and other illegal computer crimes are bright, well adjusted children. They often get good or above average grades. They enjoy the Internet and are curious about the computers connected to it. They are not trouble makers at school and are generally shy. They are either at a very advanced academic level, perhaps in a "gifted" program at school, moving at his own pace, or he is bored with school. Like every other child they are not perfect. No one would ever think they could illegally break in to a computer network and cause millions of dollars worth of damages and lost productivity.

These children are known as hackers, because the meticulously hack their why into computer networks. They generally view gaining access to these computers as challenges, and don't view themselves are criminals. The internet makes it easy for them to explore computer systems all over the world. These hackers fall into one of the following classifications:

The Novice

The novice hacker is generally inexperienced, and they are reasonably "safe" as far as hacking goes. Assuming they can even break into a system at all, they will usually simply look for games or list the files on the system they managed to break into.

The Student

Student hackers are bright, and they are bored. They are smart enough to know they have a lot to learn, and what interests them most is what they can find out next. As the name implies, this is a stage from which one can only graduate by finding out how to graduate.

This group is interested in learning as much as possible about the systems they crack. They are not interested in the data for company secrets on the system. They are interested in the computer system itself. They want to learn as much as possible about the computer environment, and then move to the next system.

The Tourist

The Tourist is out for nothing more that an adventure or the challenge of solving a puzzle. Once the Tourist gains access to a system he will do nothing more than look around for awhile and then leave.

The Crasher

The Crasher operates with little or no logical purpose. He is a trouble maker, motivated by the same elusive goals as a vandal. If it weren't for computers, he could just as easily be sprat-painting his name on the side of a building.

A Crashers only purpose is to make himself as visible as possible to his victims, and cause as much trouble as he can. He will delete files, and crash systems, with little regard for his victims.

The Thief

The Thief is the rarest form of hacker, and most hackers don't consider the Thief as hacker at all. They consider him a criminal.

The Thief is motivated by personal gain. It usually isn't money he is interested in, but data. He may be looking to steal software, or some other data the he can use or sell.

This class of "hacker" is generally the type of hacker that makes the news. The teen that breaks into the school system and changes his or other students grades, falls into the class of "hacker".

Scanners

There are programs available that your children can easily download that will scan for a computer anywhere in the world looking for vulnerabilities they can exploit and illegally access the target computer.

Scanner software does have a legitimate use by system administrators to check their systems for vulnerabilities. Unfortunately, these same programs can just as easily used to break into a system.

Computer Viruses

A computer virus is a self-replicating computer program written to alter the way a computer operates, without the permission or knowledge of the user.

Computer viruses are easily obtained on the Internet. They are dangerous to play with, especially for novices. A virus can easily escape and damage your family computer and any other computers on your home network, or it can find its way onto the Internet, effecting millions of computers.

Virus development tools are easily obtained on the internet. Software such as Virus Creation Station, or Virus Creator Pro, are sold online for as little as $20.00, as educational tools. There intent is to provide education about how viruses are developed, and how to detect them. However these same development tools can be used to create and release actual viruses on the internet.

If with the best of intentions, if one of these viruses does escape, you and your family would be responsible for the consequences. This could include financial responsibility as well as possible criminal prosecution.

Phishing

Phishers attempt to fraudulently acquire sensitive information, such as passwords and credit card details, by masquerading as a trustworthy person or business in an electronic communication.

Many children typically Phish using email to send out hundreds or even thousands of emails that appear to be from banks, or on-line payment services such as Paypal, in an attempt to lure unsuspecting people to reveal their user ID's and password. Once they have obtained someone's account information, may children will use the information to access adult web sites, or purchase items on-line.

Piracy

Computer piracy is one of the most commonly commit-ted crimes on the Internet. Many children will use Gnutella client to illegally download copyrighted music, software and movies. This is the same thing as walking into the local music store and shoplifting the latest music CD, or DVD movie.

The artist, software developers, movie writers have spend countless hours, or even years writing the music for the album, or writing computer software, or creating a script. In turn the software distributors, record and movie producers have spent millions producing, packaging and distributing the artist work, and have made is available for a reasonable fee.

Piracy cost everyone millions of dollars, in higher prices, increased law enforcement and litigation expenses. Most children don't event consider it a crime! The truth is, it is a crime that can land them in prison, and cost you a fortune in legal defense fees.

Checking your Childs Internet Activity

Computers have revolutionized communication, and in doing so have become one of the most important tools of our modern society. Computers have helped people move forward in science, medicine, business, and learning, because they let experts from anywhere the world, communicate with each other and share information. They also let other people communicate with each other, do their jobs almost anywhere, learn about almost anything, or share their opinions with each other.

The Internet is the "thing" that lets people communicate between their computers. With this ability in communications, comes great responsibility on our part as parents. Just as you want to know where your children are after school, or what they are doing at the mall, you should know where they are online.

Know Where Your Children Go

As mentioned earlier, some signs that a child might be spending too much time on the Internet or in an unhealthy e-mail or chat room relationship include, shutting the door when going online, quickly logging off when you approach, telephone calls or packages to your child from someone you don't know.

It's not difficult to find out which web sites your child has been visiting. Web browsers are designed to store a history, which shows names of sites clicked on. The key is to find the files located in your browser's history folder or cache, and just follow the bread crumbs.

Searching a computer at this level can be a difficult task if you are not comfortable searching through a computers files. I have had many fellow employees come and ask for my assistance in locating files on their home computers. Check with the Information Systems staff at your company, you may find them extremely helpful.

Web Cache

Most Web browsers are designed to cache, or store, web documents in order to reduce bandwidth usage, increase load times on frequently visited web sites, and reduce load on web servers. In its simplest form, a web cache stores copies of web pages, and images they your have previously visited.

I have provided instruction for several popular operating systems, and their default web browser. This is not a complete listing of the web browsers available, so if your child is using a different operating systems or web browser, you will need to locate where that browser stores its cache.

Windows XP

To find the cache folder in a Windows XP system, click the "Start" button, and then click on "All Programs", and then click on "Accessories", and finally "Windows Explorer".

Then on your "C" drive there should be a folder named "Documents and Settings", Click on this folder. Under this folder you should see a list of folders for each user of the computer. Click on your child's folder.

Next you will need to click on the "Tools" menu option at the top of the window, and then select "Folder Options". When the folder options window appears, select the "View" tab, and select the option "Show hidden files and folders", under "Hidden files and folders". Once you have done this click on OK.

This action should cause the folder "Local Settings" to appear. Double-Click on this folder, and then double-click on the folder "Temporary Internet Files". Finally open the file "Content". It may be "Content.IE" or something similar.

Once you are in the "Contents" folder, you should see a list of other folders with various names like, QCT1BZR3 or

38D9FO40, or some other combination of characters. These files are where Internet Explorer stores its web content and cookies. Set the folder View options to "Thumbnails" to view the content of the web site your child has been visiting.

MAC OS X

Apples Mac stores its cache is a special database file that is not accessible through traditional methods. To view the web cache on a Mac, you will need a software package call WebXTractor from InFamus Software and cost about $17.95.

Once installed, WebXTractor will allow you to search the web cache as will. You will be able to view photos, video, music and sound bytes that any user of the system has viewed.

RedHat Linux

Mozilla is the standard Web browser supplied with RedHat Linux. RedHat Linux is considerably different then Windows or Mac. First you will need the password to the root user. Once you log into RedHat you should see an Icon labeled "Home", double click on this Icon.

Once this Home directory is displayed, click once on the Up arrow on the window menu. This will display the "root", or top directory. Locate the "Home" directory file in this list and double click on it. Once the "Home" directory is displayed, you should see a list of users. Double-Click on the user whose' web cache you would like to view.

At this point, only a few files and directories will display, because most of the items in this directory are hidden. No your child is not trying to hide these files from you, they are normally hidden files. Click on the menu item "View", and then click on "Show Hidden Files". This will cause many files to be displayed.

Look for a file directory named ".Mozilla" and Double-Click on that file, then Double-Click on the file directory "Default". This will display a directory with one or maybe several file folders ending with the extension ".slt", Double-Click on one of these directories, and locate the file directory "Cache", and Double-Click on it.

You are now looking at the Web Cache for the selected user. You should see thumbnail images of any pictures or web content the user has viewed. If all you see are icons, then try clicking on the menu item "View", and then click on "Preview". An additional menu box will appear, Click on "Show Preview" at the top of the menu. The Icons in the file display window should change to thumbnails, allowing you to see the items stored in the Cache.

Browser History

Internet Explorer and Netscape along with most web browsers store a history of the sites that have been visited. In most browsers you can specify the numbers of days to keep history.

A couple of minutes reviewing the browser history can be very enlightening as to the sites your child visits. The problem with most browser histories, that they can be easily cleared. If you find that your child is regularly clearing the history, then you may want to look deeper into their online activities, as they may be trying to hide something.

Cookies

A Cookie is a piece of text sent by a server to your web browser and stored on your computer. This Cookie is then sent back by your browser each time it accesses the web page that placed to Cookie on your computer. Cookies are used for authenticating, tracking, and maintaining specific information about users, such as site preferences and the contents of an electronic shopping carts.

Cookies where designed to store information about a users login to a web site, store information for a shopping cart, and store preferences for customizable web sites. Cookies are usually stored in the users directory in a directory named "cookies", and are usually retained, even if the user clears the browser web cache. There is an option to clear cookies, but most children do not do this as they may lose access to web sites which they have managed to gain access.

A typical cookie may have a file name that contains the users' login and the name of the site. An example for this is "user@hotmail.msn[1].txt". This is a typical cookie that will indicate that your child may have an email account with Hotmail.com.

Leet Speak and Slang

Do you know what your kids are up to online? Of course you do! You've blocked all the porn sites, set up filters, and even have a monitoring program to let you know if your kids are talking about sex, or porn, or meeting up with friends in a chat room. You're a smart parent, but you'd be shocked if you knew what your children were really talking about online.

There's a new trend popular among teenage chatters, and your filters won't pick up any of it. It's called Leet Speak, or l33tspeak, net speak or just plain internet slang. Acronyms like "lol" for laugh-out-loud, "bbiab" for be back in a bit, "rofl" for rolling on floor laughing. Today's children have developed shortcuts when typing, and use single letter words: "U" replaces "you", "R" replaces "are", "o" replaces "oh", "m" replaces "am", and so on.

Less popular, but still widely used (especially in games) is true l33tspeak, which involves using numbers instead of letters. "4" replaces "A", "3" replaces "E", "7" replaces "T", "1" replaces "L", and "$" replaces "S". These are just a few examples; some of it is worse like "/\/" for "N" and "/\/\" or "M", or "13" instead of "B".

Today's children are taking their creativity to the internet, and it's affecting the way they speak. Children don't like to type much, so they try to shorten their keystrokes whenever possible. It's not only affecting the way they speak, it's starting to affect the way they write. So bad in fact, that school teachers have even reported seeing "lol" (laughing out loud) turn up on hand-written papers.

Many children as old as 17 don't know the difference between homophone such as there, their, and they're. Remember when your high school teachers used to complain about a comma splice? Today's high school teachers are struggling to teach kids how to spell, and instant messaging isn't helping.

If you're concerned about your children, it's absolutely crucial you learn to understand their language. Your filters may pick up porn, but do they catch the word "pron"? What about "warez", which is illegally obtained software.

Another key phrase is the word "paw", short for "parents are watching" or "pos" for "parents over shoulder". Every parent should be familiar with these terms. Learn to recognize the warning signs and find out what your children are doing that they don't want you to know about.

Sure you blocked porn sites, but what about Google image search? Any teenager can tell you that online image searches are the best free porn sites ever. Go ahead, Try It Just type in anything remotely dirty and see what you get.

So what can you do? Talk to your kids. Get your own copy of AOL Instant Messenger and put their names on your buddy list. Read their profiles, you may be surprised at how much personal information they a making publicly available.

Need to find out what they're up to? Try typing their screen name, email address, name, or cell phone number into Google and see what pops up. You may be surprised to find your son or daughter's picture, email address, and tons of private information about them listed on sites like "hotornot.com", "buddypic.com", "facebattle.com", "facethe-jury.com", "facebook.com" or "Myspace.com".

Does your son or daughter have a on-line journal or a blog? If so do you read it? You probably should! There's nothing wrong with reading their diary if they're posting it on the internet. Thousands of other people are reading it, why not you? How much personal information are they giving to complete strangers? You would be surprised.

Leet

Leet (or 1337) is a linguistic phenomenon associated with the underground culture centered on telecommunications, manifested primarily on the Internet. For the purposes of this text, leet is defined as the corruption or modification of written text. For example, the term "leet" itself is often written "l33t", "1337". Such corruptions are frequently referred to as "Leetspeak" or "13375p34k,". In addition to corruption of standard language, new colloquialisms have been added to the parlance. It is also important to note that Leet itself is not solely based upon one language or character set. In fact, Greek, Russian, Chinese, and other languages have been subjected to the Leet "cipher". As such, while it may be referred to as a "cipher", a "dialect", or a "language", Leet does not fit squarely into any of these categories.

The name Leet itself is derived from the word elite. Elite has been used in the past to designate a group of users as belonging to a higher social echelon than other users. Originally, "elite" had been reduced to one syllable, "'leet".

Origins of Leet

Leet finds its base in written communication over electronic media. Most simply, it has evolved as a way of forming exclusive cliques in on-line communities, notably Bulletin Board Systems and online multiplayer games, you may even see examples of Leet in video games.

One of the primary reasons Leet evolved was to circumvent text filters that block, or edit emails and text messages that contain offensive words. Parental software for example can easily filter out words such as "ass", however Leet versions of the word, such as, "455", "^55" or "/-\$$" are much more difficult to filter out.

Today's children use Leet and other various versions of it to communicate in total privacy, without the fear of parents or teachers being able to understand what they have written in emails or in a note passed in class.

Primitive Leet was generally much less elaborately substituted than modern forms. Typical transpositions included:

- exchange of "f " for "ph" as in "fone phreaks"
- exchange of "1" (one) for "l" (usually only once in a word, ie. "1iar", but not "1ist1ess")
- exchange of "k" for "c" as in "krap" as opposed to "crap", and "cill" in place of "kill"
- exchange "0" (zero) for "o" as in "0mg" instead of "omg" for "Oh my god")

Another early phenomenon was the prefix "k-" (for kilo) to some words, the most common and enduring example being "k-rad". The roots of the term "k-rad" are most likely mocking of the mid- to late-80s use of the term "radical".

As Leet grew in popularity it became even more complex and dynamic. Where originally, a one-to-one relationship existed between the source and cipher text (such as "E" for "3"), newer one-to-many and many-to-many ciphers began to emerge (such as "@" or "4" for "A", and so on).

Several outside sources have been instrumental in the formation and evolution of Leet as a dialect or cipher. Primarily, the exclusive nature of enciphering text in communities drove the evolution of the cipher. Additionally, in online games where certain text was forbidden (such as swearing, causing corruptions like "phuc" for the "F" word), newer, more clever ciphers had to be created to prevent software limitations from hindering communication. The same sort of evolution has been spurred by e-mail content filters which may prevent a user from including certain words in their "written" communication. As such, in addition to the socially exclusionary properties of using a cipher, it may be said that Leet is used as a means to defeat regular expression engines used for matching content in written communication.

Sociological Considerations

Because of the problems surrounding its lack of a spoken component, there has recently been something of a stigma attached to use of the Leet cipher. Because of its popularity with children, parenting organizations have seen fit to warn parents about the cipher. Parents, it is reasoned, may not be able to understand what their children are saying in emails, or instant messaging, and dismiss it as nonsense. It is argued that children may be discussing such nefarious things as drug use.

Despite the hurdles to attaining social acceptance, Leet has become such a part of common culture that the cipher is used even in mainstream advertising, such as the Sears Kenmore "HE4T" washing machine and dryer.

Other uses

Arguably, the first use of Leet was on the BBS's of the late 80's. On public BBS's administrators would frequently search for illegal or undesirable material, and remove them if found. As a way to combat this, users would exchange one letter for another. "Wares" would become "W4R3Z," "porn" would become "pr0n," exploits would become "3pl01tz". Leet continued to evolve in this fashion so as the new terms were picked up by administrators they were quickly replaced.

A more modern and legitimate use of leet as a cipher is computer passwords. Computer security systems often disallow the use of common English words as passwords. Leet's use as a way of ciphering English words and phrases as strings of punctuation characters can make it useful as a means of creating memorable passwords that such systems will accept. A system that will refuse "Now is the time" as a password will often be quite happy to accept "n0w157#3 71AA3".

Leet can also be used to transmit obscenities in chat room that may be monitored by automatic filtering software, or indeed any other communication intended for another human. If one is concerned that one's communications may be monitored, leet is one way of attempting to defeat this monitoring.

Similarly, simple leet is often found on websites selling or distributing pirated software or cracks, and in unwelcome of spam emails. Solicitation Leet are: W1ndOws 20OO, PhOtOsh0p, Natural Pen1s enlargement pi11$. Note that this type of leet tends to be simple and easy to read, as it is intended to foil computer filtering software but still communicate to potential customers.

Common transliterations

The Leet cipher itself is highly dynamic, and subject to stylistic interpretation. A simple list of transliterations follows:

A	B	C	D	E*	F	G	H	I*	J	K	L*	M	N	O	P	Q	R*	S	T*	U	V	W	X	Y	Z*
4	8	[	)	3	|=	6	#	1	_|	X	1	|v|	^/	0	|*	(,)	2	5	7	(_)	V	vv	><	j	2
/\	¢	<	|o	&	ph	&	/-/	!	/	|<	£	[V]	||	0	|o	0_	|?	$	+	|_|		vv	)(	'/	-/_
@	13	(	|)	|#		(_+	[-]	¿	</	}{	7	{V}	/V	oh	|o	0_	/2	z	-|-	v		'//	ecks		%
/-\	|3		|-	=-		9	|-|	i		)(	1_	em	[\]	[]	?	0_	z	ehs	1	|_|		\\'	)(		>_
^	P>	©	|=-	/=		C-	)-(	eye			|	AA	<\>	p	|^(o)	<|	|z	es	']['			\/\/			
aye	|:					gee	(-)	3y3			|_	|V|	{\}		|>		[z					(n)			
eh	!3					(V.	:-:	][				/\/\	[]\		|>		12					\/\/			
	(3					[.	|~|	]|[				(u)	//[]		|"		|2					\X/			
	/3					{.	|-|	]				(V)	/V		9							\\|/			
	)3					(.	}~[					(V)			[]D							_|_/			
							)(					/|\			|7							_:_/			
							}-(					^^													
							?					/\/|													
							}-(					/\													

* Note the use of 7 for either L or T, the use of 2 for either R or Z, the use of 3 for either E or B, and the use of 1 for either I, L, or T.

J, Q, and Y typically are not transliterated and are often used as themselves. There are some common Leet alternatives for other sounds, e.g. "ck" is often replaced with an "x" as in "hax0r" (hacker) and "sux0rs" (suckers). Sometimes an "0r" is added in place of "er".

Additionally, letters in the middle of words may be transposed. This has become the subject of some discussion in the linguistics community. People seem to be able to discern meaning from words in which the first and last morphemic letters are correctly placed, even if some of the intervening letters are incorrectly placed.

While the intentional transposition of letters in language is novel, Davis and Rawlinson have demonstrated that readers of most languages are capable of understanding the meaning of a word, provided complex phonemes and diphthongs are not corrupted. Because the meaning is easily conveyed, even with severe corruption of the original wording, the transpositions and substitutions can become quite elaborate.

Internet Slang

Internet slang is slang which Internet users have coined and consistently used. Such terms typically originated with the purpose of saving keystrokes: many use the same abbreviations in text messages. The terms often appear in lower case, with capitals often reserved for emphasis: The pronoun "I", for example, often appears simply as "i".

To avoid misapprehension and clarify the author's intent, netizens may use emoticons. Emoticons (or smilies) such as ":)" may be used both genuinely and sarcastically; for example the ":P" emoticon, can express either genuine amusement or a sense of fun, or a negative sarcastic comment on something. Deciphering and understanding what was written and what the author's intent was, is part of the Internet's attraction and enjoyment. Like most jargon, Internet slang boosts an author's apparent knowledge, causing them to appear as having specialized knowledge of an already complex medium.

Origins

The vocabulary of Internet slang (or chat speak or net speak) draws from many different sources, typically environments that placed value on brevity of communication. Some terms, such as FUBAR ("Fouled up beyond all repair") have roots as far back as World War II.

Chat acronyms originally developed on pre-Internet bulletin board systems. A handful (for example, ASAP, PO'ed) far pre-date computers. The three-letter acronym remains one of the most popular types of abbreviation in computing and telecom terminology and slang. Similar systems have since come into use with users of text-messaging wireless telephones.

With the rise of instant messaging services (ICQ, AOL, and MSN, among others) the vocabulary has expanded dramatically.

Aside from instant messaging programs another realm full of online languages exists: the Internet gaming world. One of the most popular forms of video game slang has become known as H4x0r (Haxor, meaning hacker) or as 13375p34k (in leet speak). For parents today, learning the online language can play an important role in maintaining the online safety of children.

Sometimes users make up Internet abbreviations on the spot, therefore many of them can seem confusing, obscure, whimsical, or even nonsensical. This type of on-the-spot abbreviating leads to such things as: OTP (on the phone) or the less common, OPTD (outside petting the dog). Another feature common to Internet communication involves the truncation and morphing of words that users can type more readily. Examples of this include:

- addy — "Address" (plural: "addys")
- pic — "Picture" ("pics" or "pix" for plural)
- prog — "Computer program"
- prolly — "Probably" (also "probs")
- sig — "Signature" (also "siggy")
- asl? — "Age/Sex/Location?" (also "a/s/l?"; a phrase often used in internet chat rooms)

The form "teh" offers a special case of this transformation. This originated as a corruption of "the", and often pops up spontaneously when typing fast. So common has it become, in fact, that it has made the jump to deliberate usage. Typically it occurs in situations where the writer presents as self-consciously enthusiastic, mimicking the less-grammatical Internet newbie: "That movie was teh suck!!", "The fight scene with all the Agent Smiths was TEH AWESOME". It occurs most commonly in "teh suck/orz", "teh lame," and "teh cool"..

Similarly, netizens may use the word "liek" or "leik" as sarcastic misspellings of the word "like", as in "I LIEK PIE". It often implies an insult to one's intelligence and/or typing ability. "Liek" is also often used as a geeky way of typing the preposition like, for example in the phrase "...and I was liek...".

Internet abbreviations evolve and change continually. Online games provide a good place to observe language variation in use. Often, people uninterested in computer programming do not understand the more classically "nerdy" phrases like "2B0r#2B" (which means "to be, or not to be"), thus such usages become useless or appear only in minority forums.

Common examples

Common disclaimer phrases (sometimes called "paren-theticals") also often contract into acronyms — they tend to occur at certain points in a sentence, which can facilitate decoding. By far the most common of these are "lol", "lmao", "rofl", "omg", "brb" and "iws". This is a fraction of the full list, but some of these disclaimers include:

- AFK: away from keyboard
- AFAIK: as far as I know
- ASAP: as soon as possible
- ATM: at the moment
- Bai2u: 'bye to you' goodbye
- BBIAB: be back in a bit (used to express a longer time of absence than with "brb")
- BBL: be back later
- BBS: be back soon
- BRB: be right back or bathroom break (very commonly used)
- BTW: by the way
- Bump: used in forums to bring a post to the top of the forum list (a common acronym for "bring up my post")

- CYA: see ya, or see you later (also CU) (or, less commonly and depending on the context, cover your ass)
- DMY: don't mess yourself (used to tell someone they are overreacting, seen on "The Simpson's" as a spoken abbreviation)
- DW: Don't Worry
- F2P: free to play
- F2F: Face to Face
- FTL: for the lose (used to dislike something)
- FTW: for the win (used to express enthusiasm or approval)
- FYI: for your information
- FYSIWALOL: finding your saying interesting without actually laughing out loud
- G2G or GTG: got to go or good to go
- GG: good game or good god
- GF: Good Fight
- GJ: Good Job
- GL: good luck
- GN8: good night
- GTH: go to hell
- GOOMH: Get Out Of My House
- GLLN: Got Laid Last Night(?)
- Hai2u: 'hi to you' hello
- HOMG: Ho my God
- HTH: hope that helps or happy to help
- IANAL: I am not a lawyer (used when offering amateur commentary on a legal case)
- IAS: I am smiling (not quite "lol")
- IDK: I don't know
- IIRC: if I recall/remember correctly

- IMO: in my opinion
- IMHO: in my humble/honest opinion (derived from IMO or vice-versa)
- IRL: in real life
- IWS: I want sex
- JIC: just in case
- JK: just kidding
- JW: just wondering
- KIT: keep in touch
- KK: okay
- kthxbye: Shorter, and faster, way of saying "Okay. thank you. Good bye".
- Lag: where a connection is not as fast as others making the game lag behind
- L33t: elite
- LFG: looking for group (used mostly in MMORPGs)
- LFT: looking for team (used mostly in MMORPGs)
- LOL: laugh out loud
- LMAO: Laugh my ass off
- L2P: learn to play
- LYLAS: love you like a sister
- nOOb: Newbie, often one who dies alot in their first few times in games online
- N1: nice one
- NP: no problem
- NS: nice shot
- NT: nice try
- NVM: never mind
- NSFW: not safe for work (often used as a warning that a link contains racy or pornographic images)
- NWS: not work safe

- OAC: Only At Croons
- OMG: oh my god
- OMGWTFBBQ: combines the terms OMG, WTF, and BBQ. (can also be used as a mockery of newbie's who express surprise at commonly known facts, or in self deprecation)
- OMW: on my way (usually used in ORPGs)
- OH NOES: oh no
- OP: original post/original poster (referring to the first post in a thread)
- OTOH: on the other hand
- ORV: orita vengo (used in Spanish)
- P2P: pay to play, player to player, or peer to peer
- PK: Player kill
- POS: Parent over Shoulder
- PVP: Player vs. Player
- PVE: Player vs. Enemy/Environment
- PWN: (p)owned. Usually referring to someone in a video game being decidedly beaten by another player.
- PEBKAC: problem exists between keyboard and chair
- QFT: quoted for truth
- QQ: cry more (meant to look like eyes with tears dripping from them)
- QT: cutie
- RE: returned or back or rematch
- RM: remake
- ROFL: rolling on floor laughing
- ROFLCOPTER: retardation of ROFLMAO
- ROTFL: rolling on the floor laughing
- SGTM: Silently giggling to myself
- SFW: safe for work

- SIF: As if
- SU: shut up
- STBU: Sucks to be you
- STHU: shut the hell up
- TBA: to be added or to be announced
- TBH: to be honest
- TT4N: ta ta for now
- TTYL: talk to you later
- TTYS: talk to you soon
- TY: thank you
- TYVM: thank you very much
- THX: thanks
- YW: you're welcome
- WB: Welcome back
- W/E(W\E)(W.E)(WE): whatever
- WD: Well done
- WS: work safe
- WTH: what the heck/hell
- WTB: want to buy
- WTG: way to go
- WTT: want to trade
- WTV: watching tv
- WUU2: what you up to
- WU@: where you at

Spam

Spam is the abuse of electronic messaging systems to send unsolicited, bulk messages. While the most widely recognized form of spam is e-mail spam, the term is applied to similar abuses in other media: instant messaging spam, Usenet newsgroup spam, Web search engine spam, spam in blogs, and mobile phone messaging spam.

Why do companies send spam? Because it is economically viable for advertisers since it effectively has no operating costs beyond the management of their mailing lists, and it has proved difficult to hold senders accountable for their mass mailings. Because the barrier to entry is so low, spammers are numerous and the volume of unsolicited mail has become very high. The costs, such as lost productivity and fraud, are borne by the public and by Internet service providers, which add extra capacity to cope with the deluge. Spamming is widely reviled, and has been the subject of legislation in many jurisdictions.

Many people have asked me how spammers get their email address. They tell me that are very careful about using their email address, and only provide their email to people they know. The fact is, the more active they are on the Internet, the more likely it is their email address will be available to the masses.

Spammers have numerous methods for obtaining email addresses, from simple purchasing it, to guessing it. Spammers routinely harvest many sources for valid email addresses.

e-Mail Harvesting

E-mail harvesting is the process of obtaining lists of e-mail addresses for use in bulk mail or other purposes usually grouped as spam. Methods range from purchasing lists of e-mail addresses from other spammers to the more common use of special software, known as "harvesting software", "harvesting bots" or "harvesters", which scan web pages, postings on Usenet, mailing list archives and other online sources to obtain e-mail addresses.

It is important to realize that just because you or your children received spam, whether it's to purchase medication online, buy a watch, or an invitation to visit an adult web site, doesn't mean you have to have visited one of those sites to end up on their email list.

Listed here are some common methods used by spammers to obtain email addresses, possibly yours included.

From Email Lists

An Email list is a type of Internet forum, and is a special usage of e-mail that allows for widespread distribution of information to many Internet users. With an email list, people can subscribe to received email about a specific topics or events.

Spammers regularly attempt to get the lists of subscribers to mailing lists. Some mail servers will provide a complete list of subscribers upon request, knowing that the email addresses are generally correct and only a few of the addresses are invalid. Once they obtain the list of email addresses they begin to forward all types of spam.

From Web Pages

Spammers have programs which scan through web pages, looking for email addresses. Some web pages contain an HTML tag called "Mailto:" that contain email addresses that spammers can extract.

From a Web Browser

Some sites use various tricks to extract a surfer's email address from the web browser, sometimes without the surfer noticing it.

Web page developers write web pages that are designed to extract information from your web browser. Some information that they need is legitimate. The type of web browser you are using, or the display size of your screen are valid pieces of information they commonly extract so that they can accurately display web pages.

However, in additional to this information they can also extract your email address from your web browser.

It should also be noted that when you read your e-mail from a web browser, or any email reader that understands HTML, such as Outlook, you should be aware of active content. Active content is a web page that uses JavaScript, or Visual Basic to perform various tasks.

An E-mail containing HTML may contain a script that upon being read, or even the subject being highlighted, can automatically send an E-mail to another E-mail addresses. A good example of this is the "Melissa virus", which on March 29, 1999 shutdown most email systems on a global basis. Such a script could send the spammer not only your e-mail address but all the addresses in your address book.

IRC and Chat rooms

Some IRC (Internet Relay Chat) clients will give a user's email address to anyone who cares to ask it. Many spammers harvest email addresses from IRC, knowing that those are 'live' addresses and send spam to those email addresses.

This is another major source of email addresses for spammers, especially as this is one of the first public activities newbie's join, making it easy for spammers to harvest 'fresh' addresses of people who might have very little experience dealing with spam.

AOL chat rooms are the most popular of those. Spammers have software that extracts the screen names of participants in AOL chat rooms. AOL is targeted for two main reasons, first AOL makes the list of the actively participating users' screen names available and, second AOL users are considered prime targets by spammers due to the reputation of AOL as being the Internet Service Provider (ISP) of choice by newbie's.

Finger Daemons

A finger daemon is a specialized program that provides the status of a user connected to a particular computer. System administrators generally use this feature to confirm who a particular user is, where they maybe located, and if they are currently connected.

Some finger daemons are very friendly. A finger query asking for john@host.com will produce a list of information about John, including all information contained in that users account record. This could include his full name, address, and phone number. In some cases just sending a finger query to '@host.com' will produce a list of all active users on the specified host.

Spammers can then use this information to get extensive user lists from hosts, of active accounts, that will read their mail soon enough to be really attractive spam targets.

From domain contact points

Every domain on the internet has one to three contact points, administration, technical, and billing. The contact point includes the email address of the contact person that owns that domain.

As the contact points are freely available, using the 'whois' command, spammers harvest the email addresses from the contact points for lists of domains. A list of all domains on the internet is made available to the public by the domain registries. This is a tempting methods for spammers, as those email addresses are most usually valid and mail sent them is being read regularly.

Guessing and Cleaning

Some spammers guess email addresses, and send a spam message to a list of email address that have been guessed. Then they wait for either an error message to return by email, indicating that the email address is incorrect, or for a confirmation. A confirmation is easily solicited by inserting non-standard but commonly used email headers requesting that the delivery system, the email client, send a confirmation of delivery.

Guessing is generally based on the fact that email addresses are based on people's names, usually in commonly used ways, first.last@domain or an initial of one name followed or proceeded by the other and by adding the @domain extension.

Also, some email addresses are standard, "postmaster" is mandated for internet email. Other common email addresses are "postmaster", "hostmaster", and "root" on nearly all UNIX based systems.

Social Engineering

This method means the spammer uses a hoax to convince people into giving them valid e-mail addresses.

A good example was Richard Douche's "Free CD's" chain letter. Richard sent an email promising a free CD for every person to whom the letter is forwarded to as long as it is CC'ed or copied to Richard.

Richard claimed to be associated with Amazon and Music Blvd, among other companies, who authorized him to make this offer. Yet he supplied no references to web pages and used a free e-mail address. All Richard wanted was to get people to send him valid e-mail addresses in order to build a list of addresses to spam and/or sell.

By creating an email that people would quickly forward because of the possibility of receiving a free CD, Richard was able to obtain millions of email addresses for his spam list.

Buying lists from Others

In this category, there are two types of trades. The first type consists of buying a list of email addresses, often on CD, that were harvested via other methods, perhaps someone harvesting email addresses from UseNet and sells the list either to a company that wishes to advertise via email, some-times passing off the list as that of people who opted-in for emailed advertisements, or to others who resell the list.

The second type consists of a company who got the email addresses legitimately, such as a magazine that asks subscribers for their email in order to keep in touch over the Internet, and sells the list for the extra income.

How to avoid getting spammed

Don't give out your email address. I know that's easier said than done. But the more you distribute your email, the more likely it will make its way to a spam list.

There is no way to avoid spam entirely, but there are steps you can take to reduce the chances of your email address showing up on some companies spam list.

Many spammers use programs called web crawlers that scan millions of web pages every day looking for email addresses that have been posted to a web page.

Because of these web crawlers, it is advisable that you do not put you or your child's email address on a personal web page. Many people think it would be nice to receive email from people viewing their web page, but doing so it like placing a billboard on the side of the highway with your email address on it.

Do not post messages to Usenet Newsgroups. Spammers regularly use scanning software to extract the email address of those that post message to Newsgroups. Spammers will generally categorize these email addresses obtained from Newsgroups, based on the subject of the Newsgroup. For example, email addresses extracted from "alt.movie.reviews" may be sent spam related to movies rentals, while someone whose posts messages to "stamps.collecting" will receive email about collectables, and those who post messages to the group "alt.sex.abuse.recovery" may receive email promoting pornographic web sites.

Do not allow your child to use his email address on web site offering free music, downloads, or anything else if they register their email address. These lists of often sold to spammers. Generally the software or download the web site is offering is publicly available software known as freeware or shareware, and can be located easily without giving someone your email address.

How to Curtail your current spam

Once the deluge of unsolicited email start, it is nearly impossible to stop. There are several things you can try to help reduce the amount of unwanted email you receive, but you will never eliminate it.

Do not replay to an unsolicited email. Even it the email has the statement, "To be removed from this email list, please send and email to the following email address, and place the word REMOVE in the subject line" Doing so will simply confirm that they have a valid email address. Sure they may not send you another email, but they will sell your email address to as many spammers as they can, and those spammers will send more spam.

Check with your Internet Service Provider. Most are very sensitive about spam. These spam emails place a huge strain on the ISP's email servers. If the ISP can limit or eliminate these spam emails, then their own servers will work more efficiently, and will ultimately reduce their operating cost, which in turn keep your costs down.

If your ISP requests a copy of the spam email, then make sure they receive the entire email, including the email headers. The header will allow the ISP to determine where the spam originated, and will help them filter out any future spam that spammer sends.

Many email programs will allow you to setup filters. Learn to configure the filters in the email program you use. These filters can be very effective. But be warned, some can be very time consuming to setup.

Software Tools

Software tool are everywhere these days. They can be found as shareware that promotes copying and sharing the software with a friend, or from the local office supply store, and is available in a range of prices, depending on features and complexity.

In this chapter I will introduce you to several different types of software that is designed to help protect your children from on-line predators.

Antivirus Software

There are an estimated 150,000 computer viruses in existence today, with as many as 200 new viruses being detected every month. It is therefore mandatory that you protect your computer systems from these treats.

Computer viruses come in many forms, ranging from simple but annoying popup messages, to complete attacks that destroy your computer files.

Not all malicious software is a virus. In order for a computer program to be considers a virus, it must have the ability to spread itself from one system to another. Therefore many viruses use e-mail to spread themselves to other systems.

Besides malware, viruses, worms, and Trojan horse's there are many other factors out there that can affect your computer. Antivirus software is designed to intercept these treats and prevent damage to your system. Listed here are a some of the more common treats that antivirus software may prevent.

Malware

Malware is software designed to infiltrate and damage a computer system, without the owner's consent. The term is a combination "mal-" for "malicious" and "-ware" from "software", and describes the intent of the creator, rather than any particular feature. Malware is commonly taken to include computer viruses, and worms. Strictly speaking however, malware is any software designed to cause harm to the data stored on a computer system.

Worms

A computer worm is a self-replicating computer program similar to a computer virus. A virus attaches itself to, and becomes part of another executable program, however a worm is self-contained and does not need to be part of another program to propagate itself. Worms are often designed to exploit the file transmission capabilities found on many computers, such as e-mail or Instant Messaging. The main difference between a computer virus and a worm is that a virus cannot propagate by itself whereas worms can. A worm uses a network to send copies of itself to other systems and it does so without any intervention. In general, worms harm the network by consuming bandwidth, whereas viruses infect or corrupt files on a targeted computer. Viruses generally do not affect network performance, as their nefarious activities are mostly confined within the target computer itself.

Trojan Horse

A Trojan horse is a malicious program that is disguised as, or embedded into legitimate software. The term is derived from the classical myth of the Trojan horse in which the Greeks gained entrance to the city of Troy by hiding inside of a giant wooden horse presented to the Trojans as a gift. In the same fashion, software can be hidden inside an ordinary program, perhaps a games or other tame looking program. When the user starts the program however, the hidden code may be unlocking secure files, deleting system files, or loading other viruses onto the computer.

There are two common types of Trojan horses. One, is otherwise useful software that has been corrupted by a cracker inserting malicious code that executes while the program is used. Examples include various implementations of weather alerting programs, computer clock setting software, and peer to peer file sharing utilities such as Gnuttella.

The other type is a standalone program that masquerades as something else, like a game or image file, in order to trick the user into some using the software so that it may carry out its objective.

Trojan horse programs cannot operate autonomously, in contrast to some other types of malware, like viruses or worms. Just as the Greeks needed the Trojans to bring the horse inside for their plan to work, Trojan horse programs depend on actions by the intended victims. As such, if Trojans replicate and even distribute themselves, each new victim must run the Trojan horse program. Therefore their virulence is of a different nature, depending on successful implementation of social engineering concepts rather than flaws in a computer system's security design or configuration.

Logic Bombs

A logic bomb is a piece of code intentionally inserted into a software system that will set off a malicious function when specified conditions are met. For example, a programmer may hide a piece of code that starts deleting files, should he ever leave his employer. When his payroll record indicates a termination date, the logic bomb may begin deleting or corrupting files only he knows how to fix.

Software that is inherently malicious, such as viruses and worms, often contain logic bombs that execute a certain payload at a pre-defined time or when some other condition is met. This technique can be used by a virus or worm to gain momentum and spread before being noticed. Many viruses attack their host systems on specific dates, such as Friday the 13th or April Fool's Day. Trojans that activate on certain dates are often called "time bombs".

Back doors

On Windows computers, three viruses are commonly used by intruders to gain remote access to your computer. They are BackOrifice, Netbus, and SubSeven, and once installed, on your system allow other people to access and control your computer.

Denial of service

Another form of attack is called a denial-of-service (DoS) attack. This type of attack causes your computer to crash or to become so busy processing data that you are unable to use it. In most cases, the latest patches will prevent the attack.

Another aspect of this type of attack is to note that in addition to being the target of a DoS attack, it is possible for your computer to be used as a participant in a denial-of-service attack. To use your system in such an attack, intruders will frequently use compromised computers as launching pads for attacking other systems. An example of this is how distributed denial-of-service (DDoS) tools are used. The intruders install an "agent", frequently through a Trojan horse program, that runs on the compromised computer awaiting further instructions. Then, when a number of agents are running on different computers, a single "handler" can instruct all of them to launch a denial-of-service attack on another system. Thus, the end target of the attack is not your own computer, but someone else's computer, your computer is just a convenient tool in a larger attack.

Unprotected Windows Network shares

A Windows networking share is the result of someone sharing a directory on their computer with no security.

These unprotected networking shares can be exploited by intruders to place "agents" on large numbers of Windows-based computers attached to the Internet. Because site security on the Internet is interdependent, a compromised computer not only creates problems for the computer's owner, but it is also a threat to other sites on the Internet. The greater immediate risk to the Internet community is the potentially large number of computers attached to the Internet with unprotected Windows networking shares combined with distributed attack tools.

Mobile code

Mobile code is software obtained from a remote systems transferred across a network, and then downloaded and executed on a local system without explicit installation or execution by the recipient. An example of mobile code is a Flash animations, or Shockwave movies that you may view on the Web, commonly used on Myspace.com.

There have been reports of problems with "mobile code" to run malicious code on your computer without your knowledge.

Also be aware of the risks involved in the use of mobile code within email programs. Many email programs use the same code as web browsers. Thus, vulnerabilities that affect your web browser are often applicable to email as well.

Cross-site scripting

A malicious web developer may attach a script to something sent to a web site, such as a URL, an element in a form, or a database inquiry. Later, when the web site responds to your request, the malicious script is transferred to your browser.

You can potentially expose your web browser to malicious scripts by following links in web pages, email messages, or newsgroup postings without knowing what they link to using interactive forms on an untrustworthy site, viewing online discussion groups, forums, or other dynamically generated pages where users can post text containing HTML tags.

Chat clients

Internet chat applications, such as instant messaging applications and Internet Relay Chat (IRC) networks, provide a mechanism for information to be transmitted bi-directionally between computers on the Internet. Chat clients provide groups of individuals with the means to exchange dialog, web URLs, and in many cases, files of any type.

Because many chat clients allow for the exchange of executable code, they present risks similar to those of email clients. As with email clients, care should be taken to limit the chat client's ability to execute downloaded files. As always, you should be wary of exchanging files with unknown parties.

Packet sniffers

A packet sniffer is a program that captures data from information packets as they travel over the network. That data may include user names, passwords, and proprietary information that travels over the network in clear text. With perhaps hundreds or thousands of passwords captured by the packet sniffer, intruders can launch widespread attacks on systems.

Relative to DSL and traditional dial-up users, cable modem users have a higher risk of exposure to packet sniffers since entire neighborhoods of cable modem users are effectively part of the same Local Area Network (LAN.) A packet sniffer installed on any cable modem user's computer in your neighborhood may be able to capture data transmitted by any other cable modem in the same neighborhood.

Email spoofing

Email "spoofing" is when an email message appears to have originated from one source when it actually was sent from another source. Email spoofing is often an attempt to trick the user into making a damaging statement or releasing sensitive information, such as passwords.

Spoofed email can range from harmless pranks to social engineering ploys.

Examples of the latter include:

- Email claiming to be from a system administrator requesting users to change their passwords to a specified string and threatening to suspend their account if they do not comply.

- Email claiming to be from a person in authority requesting users to send them a copy of a password file or other sensitive information.

- Email claiming to be from a service such as EBay, claiming that you own money, or money is owed to you. This email may appear to be from the service provider, but when you click on the link in the email you are sent to a bogus login that looks like the service providers web page.

Note that while service providers may occasionally request that you change your password, they usually will not specify what you should change it to. Also, legitimate service providers will never ask you to verify your personal information, user ID and password. If you suspect that you may have received a spoofed email from someone with malicious intent, you should contact your service provider's support personnel immediately.

Email borne viruses

Viruses and other types of malicious code are often spread as attachments to email messages. Before opening any attachments, be sure you know the source of the attachment. It is not enough that the mail originated from an address you recognize. The Melissa virus spread precisely because it originated from a familiar address. Also, malicious code might be distributed in amusing or enticing programs attached to emails, such as funny games.

Never run a program unless you know it to be authored by a person or company that you trust. Also, don't send programs of unknown origin to your friends or coworkers simply because they are amusing. They might contain a Trojan horse program, and it may be traced to your email address as the originator.

Hidden file extensions

Windows operating systems contain an option to "Hide file extensions for known file types". The option is enabled by default, but a user may choose to disable this option in order to have file extensions displayed by Windows. Multiple email-borne viruses are known to exploit hidden file extensions. The first major attack that took advantage of a hidden file extension was the VBS/LoveLetter worm which contained an email attachment named "LOVE-LETTER-FOR-YOU.TXT.vbs". Other malicious programs have since incorporated similar naming schemes.

Examples include:

- Downloader (MySis.avi.exe or Quick-Flick.mpg.exe)
- Timofonica (TIMOFONICA.TXT.vbs)
- CoolNote (COOL_NOTEPAD_DEMO.TXT.vbs)
- OnTheFly (AnnaKournikova.jpg.vbs)

The files attached to the email messages sent by these viruses may appear to be harmless text (.txt), or Videos (.mpg and .avi) or other file types when in fact the file is a malicious script or executable (.vbs or .exe, for example). Simply double-clicking on these files to view the "picture" or "video" causes the program to be executed, causing all types of unknown problems.

Parental Control Software

Parental control software is a term for content-filtering software, especially when it is used to filter content delivered over the Web. Content-control software determines what content will be available on a particular machine or network. The motive is often to protect children or to prevent employees from viewing non-work-related sites. Pornography, gambling, alternative lifestyles, sexuality, political content, and religious web sites may be filtered. Content-control software can also be used to block Internet access entirely.

Many companies offer Parental control software, and each has its strong points and its weaknesses. I recommend that you research the various applications available, and weigh them against your values, and what you are willing to spend.

Presented here is a list, in alphabetical order, of several very popular applications. Each one is perfectly capable of providing protection from unwanted content. I am not promoting any particular application, but I can not possibly list all the applications here, as there are too many to list.

- Child Safe
- Cyber Patrol
- Content Protect
- Cyber Sentinel
- Cyber Sitter
- Cyber Snoop
- Filter Pak
- McAfee Parental Control
- Net Nanny
- Norton Parental Control

Key Loggers

Key loggers are a type of diagnostic tool used in software development that captures the user's keystrokes. It can be useful to determine sources of errors in software applications. Such systems are also highly useful for law enforcement as well as espionage. For instance, installing a Key Logger on a suspects PC may provide a means to obtain passwords or encryption keys and thus bypassing other security measures. However, key loggers are widely available on the internet and can be used by anyone for the same purpose.

Search Engine Filters

Some search engines, such as Google, allow the user to specify specific preferences, including filtering out objectionable content and images.

These features vary in effectiveness from site to site, and most do not provide much in the area of security, so your children could easily change these preferences without your knowledge.

Your ISP as a Filter

Check with your ISP and see if they offer internet content filtering or any other parental controls, as many ISP's are offering content filtering as part of a package or as a separate add-on to your account.

The advantage of having your ISP handling the filtering of your internet connection is that it makes it much more difficult for anyone to bypass the filters. Additionally, all computers connected to your home network will benefit from the service, reducing the likely hood of objectionable content, and/or sites from popping up on any of your home PC's.

AOL Parental Controls

For the most part, AOL has done a good job with their parental controls. If you are an AOL subscriber, learn to use these controls and make sure you use them on your child's AOL account.

Do not give your child access to the primary AOL screen name, as he will be able to change or remove the parental control from his account.

AOL allows you to create multiple screen names for each of your children, and then through the primary screen name, you can maintain various parental controls on each child, each with more or less restrictions as their ages warrant.

Activity Monitors

Activity monitors are different than Parent control software, as they generally do not filter, or block access to web sites or content, rather they record what someone does online, however some do have limited blocking capabilities.

Some activity monitors such as WebWatcher, record all key strokes, snapshots of web content, and record both sides of Instant Message conversations, as well as e-mail, and it can even record some offline activities.

Problems with Tools

The primary drawback with parental control software, it that it often becomes a battle of wits for most teens to figure out how to bypass the software, and in many cases, the teens will figure it out.

Ironically, the one tool children need in order to figure out how to bypass content filter software is the internet itself. There are extensive web sites that teach children how to bypass almost any content filtering software application. These sites are generally not blocked, and teens can easily locate the information they need.

Some of the techniques I have found on the web are:

- Many teens use circumvention sites – Teens usually locate these sites with ease.

- There are e-mail lists that children can subscribe that send out emails, announcing new Circumventor sites every 3 or 4 days. These sites change often because blocking software companies have also subscribed to these lists and add these sites to the lists of blocked sites.

- If you have a computer with an uncensored Internet connection, children can easily set up there own Circumventor site. For example, if your child has a friend with an uncensored Internet connection, he can install the Circumventor software on his friends' home computer. The software will then give him a him a new web address that he can take home with him and type it into his browser at home to get around the network blocking software. This will allow him to surf from his friend computer remotely.

- Other children use a program called "Ubuntu Live". This software creates a CD that your child can use to reboot their computer with a whole new operating system that has no blocking software at all. They will be free to surf the web completely unrestricted. When they are done surfing the web, they simply remove the CD, and reboot the computer.

- Other sites list methods for deleting or clearing the content filters logs, so parents will not be able to tell what sites they have visited or tried to visit.

- I have also founds many suggestions for bypassing the AOL parental controls. According to the web sites I have found, many methods have been tried with varying success.

Email Tracing

Email tracing is relatively easy because of how email travels on the internet. As email travels from computer to computer, the email gathers information about each computer it comes in contact with. This information is stored in what are referred to as the email headers.

The email header is vital in determining where an email originated. If you ever receive a harassing or threatening email, be sure to preserve the email on your system. Most email systems do not print the header when you send the email to the printer. The police will need the email along with its complete headers in order to trace the email back to its origin.

Since it is relatively easy to generate an email that appears to have originated from a friend, or relative, it is very difficult to falsify the original of the email contained in the headers.

This is the reason many spammers use virus software to take control of a victims computer, and send massive amounts of spam from hijacked PC's. By doing this the emails end up being traced to the hijacked IP Address, allowing spammers to continue to send unwanted spam all over the world.

Communication

The Internet has provided some wonderful opportunities for our children. Never before have children had access to such a powerful tool for conducting school research, learning about new things, finding new recreation and entertainment, and communicating with their friends both around the corner and around the globe.

However, children are uniquely at risk online, and for them, surfing the Internet can sometimes be like walking down a dark street all alone.

As a parent, you've probably thought at some point that your children know more about the Internet than you do, and to a degree, you're right. Growing up with the technology, children sometimes adapt to the Internet much more rapidly than adults. Having experience with the computer and the Internet is not the same thing as having experience in life. Children are all the more threatened online because they often lack understanding of the motives and intentions of others, and do not realize the danger in which they may place themselves and their families by giving away personal information about themselves.

Children have a rich private life away from adults, and in some ways that can be a good thing. The key to protecting your child online is to stay involved in their use of the Internet, and to be aware of their online activities. Children need to be granted some responsibility in order to develop, and the Internet is no exception. But just as you wouldn't send your children on to the streets of some strange city all by themselves, you shouldn't leave them online without parental guidance. Encourage your children to tell you about any online experience that scares or upsets them, then discuss the experience with your child.

Tips for parents

Talk to your children about the dangers lurking on the internet. Let them know that not everyone on the internet is telling the truth. Make them aware that the 13 year old child they may be talking to, could really be a 40 year old pedophile trying extract information from them.

Young children shouldn't use chat rooms! The dangers are too great. As children get older, direct them towards well-monitored child friendly chat rooms. Monitored chat room are generally monitored by a responsible party, which has the ability to eject or kick offending participants out of the chat room if they violate the rules.

Inform your child to never give out personal information, such as name, address, phone number, school name or pictures. You should also stress to your children that they should not give out personal information about their friends either. It is just as bad is giving out their own personal information. Pedophiles often obtain information about a potential victim, by questions his friends, who are usually very willing to talk about someone else in great detail.

If at all possible, keep the computer is a room other than the child's bedroom so you can monitor what your child is doing. If your child is older, or there is no other place other than the child's bedroom, make sure the bedroom rooms door is open, not just unlocked, but opened, so that you can monitor their activity.

Make sure that you understand the services, and the software your child will be using on the internet. Discuss with them what these services are and how they are used.

Make sure you install blocking software and discuss it with your child. Let them know that the software is there for their protection, and that it will log all their activity.

For places outside your supervision, such as the public library, school media center, or a friends home, find out what computer safeguards are used.

Spend time surfing the internet with your child, so that you can set a good example for online behavior. It will also get your child used to the fact that you are watching, and are aware of what they are doing.

Inform your children never to respond to threatening or offensive messages, or emails, as these may be lures to open a dialog to learn more about your child. Scammers, predators and identify thieves will often send blanket emails to millions of email addresses harvested from Usenet news-groups, or chat rooms, or randomly generated. They generally do not know if the email address they are sending to is even valid. However, if your child response to the email, then they have a confirmation that your email is valid, and will quickly begin bombarding your email with spam.

When discussing your child's day, be sure to ask about the time they spent online. This keeps them aware that you are actively monitoring their activities, and as a result they will become used to keeping you up-to-date on their activities.

Discuss with your child that they should never meet anyone they have meet online without your permission and without your presence. Inform them that there are people out in the real world that would have no problem hurting them, or kidnapping them.

If your child is talking to someone online, make sure you learn as much as possible about the person, and make sure the topic of the discussions are age appropriate.

Encourage your children to inform you of any mes-sages, emails or web sites that make them uncomfortable or frighten them, so they you can take appropriate steps to resolve the issue. This may be updating monitoring software, or having a discussion with your child about what has hap-pened.

Once you have discussed these things with your child, set up an internet usage policy that covers usage guidelines, and schedules and durations.

Policies

Most businesses have established internet usage policies for their employees. These policies establish what is permitted and what is not permitted on a company's network. These policies usually go further and establish penalties for misuse of the network, and violation of the company policies. These policies often include termination of employment or even criminal prosecution.

If you are going to allow your children to access the internet, then you should have an internet usage policy that also establishes the rules. This policy should also establish the penalties for violation of the policies. If your child violates the policies you have established, then perhaps loss of computer access, or no Internet access for a period of time will be adequate.

In my house, I use a router to control internet access, so if I need to suspend someone's internet access, I can simple login to my router using the Administrators login on the router, and restrict the particular Childs' computer from accessing the internet. They still have access to the home network, so printing out homework assignments is still possible.

Depending on the age of your children, you may need multiple usage policies tailored to specific age groups. For younger children, say under 13, you may simply need a list of "Do's and Don'ts", with a list of penalties for breaking the rules. While for older children, say ages 13 and older, you may need a more extensive policy, with additional considerations.

On the following pages are, two basic templates for Internet usage policies, for each age groups discussed.

Policy for Young Children

Just as you teach your children to follow safety rules for talking to strangers or crossing the street, and to brush their teeth and tie their shoes, you should teach them how to stay safe while surfing the Internet.

Establish the following:

- Decide how long and when your child can use the computer and Internet each day.

- If possible, set up the computer in a common area so that you see what's going on.

- Let your child know that you have a right to see what's on the screen, and in his/her email.

- Talk to your child about sites visited, with whom they've conversed, and what topics were discussed.

- Familiarize yourself with your child's favorite sites. Make sure any chat rooms your child visits are monitored, live, by adults.

- Travel the Internet with your child. Bookmark safe sites for your child to visit.

- Install Internet monitoring software as discussed under Software Tools.

The Rules

- DO tell your parents right away about anything online that makes you feel uncomfortable.

- DO be polite, and use proper language while online.

- DON'T give out personal information – Name, address including the city you live, telephone number, school name or location, without your parents' permission. This includes sites like MySpace.com. Armed with a picture and the name of your school, it is easy for predators to locate you.

- DON'T agree to meet someone you met online. Tell your parents if someone does ask to meet you some place. If your parents agree to meet the person, make sure your parents are with you at all times.

- DON'T send anyone your picture without your parents' permission.

- DON'T post your picture on a site such as MySpace.com with out your parent's permission.

- DON'T respond to any messages that are mean or cause you to feel bad. Tell your parents right away.

- DON'T give out your Internet password to anyone but your parents.

Policy for Teens

The Internet is an electronic highway connecting millions of computers all over the world and hundreds of millions of individual subscribers. The key concept underlying the Internet is interconnectivity, something that will allow you to access an unparalleled array of communication and information resources.

Internet access is coordinated through a complex association of government agencies, and regional and state networks. In addition, the smooth operation of the network relies upon the proper conduct of the end users who must adhere to strict guidelines. In general, this requires efficient, ethical, and legal utilization of the network resources. Failure to follow these policies may result in your loss of internet access. Your signature at the end of this Internet Use Agreement acknowledges that you will follow these policies.

Internet - Terms and Conditions

1. Acceptable Use - The purpose of the Internet is to support research and education for school, and your access to the Internet is provided for that purpose. Any use of the Internet to transmit, download, upload, or duplicate any copyrighted materials (including, but not limited to, software, music, publications and graphics), or materials protected by applicable copyright laws is prohibited. Use of another organization's network or computing resources must comply with the rules appropriate for that network. Transmission of any material in violation of any U.S. or state regulation is prohibited. Users shall not transmit, download, upload,

duplicate or create any threatening or obscene materials. You shall not purchase items via the Internet, subscribe to commercial services such as, but not limited to, bulletin boards, or chat groups without approval from your parents or guardian.

2. Privileges - The use of the Internet is a privilege, not a right, and inappropriate use will result in the cancellation of those privileges. Your parents will deem what is appropriate use and their decision is final. You shall not attempt to gain access to the computer under any name or password other than the one issued to you by your parents.

3. Network Etiquette - You are expected to abide by the generally accepted rules of network etiquette. These include, but are not limited to the following:

- Be polite. Do not be abusive in your messages to others. Use English or other acceptable household language. Use of Leet speak, coded messages or other internet short hand will not be tolerated.

- Use appropriate language. Do not swear, use vulgarities or any other inappropriate language. Illegal activities are strictly forbidden.

- Users should not reveal personal address, phone numbers or social security number, name of school, personal pictures, or personal information about themselves, friends of other family members.

- Electronic mail (E-mail) and other materials created by you are not private. There will be no expectation of privacy for any materials created, copied, downloaded, or accessed by you on any computer or workstation including printouts of such materials. Your parents will have complete access to all materials on any system including E-mail.

- Do not use the network in such a way that would disrupt the use of the network for other users.

- All communications and information accessible via the network must be assumed to be the private property of the author and may not be downloaded, copied, or used without the author's permission.

4. Warranties – Your parents make no guarantees of any kinds for your access to the Internet, and your access is at your parent's soles discretion.

5. Security - Security on any computer system is a high priority, especially when the system involves personal family information. If you identify a security problem on the Internet you must notify your parents. You may not demonstrate the problem to other users. Attempts to log in to the family computer, network or Internet as a system administrator or under a user name other than the one given to you will result in cancellation of your privileges or other disciplinary action.

6. Vandalism - Vandalism will result in cancellation of your internet privileges or other disciplinary action. Vandalism is defined as any malicious attempt to harm or destroy data of another user, the Internet, and/or other networks that are connected to the Internet. This includes, but is not limited to, the intentional uploading or creation of computer viruses, or any illegal or improper use of the Internet or accessed equipment.

7. Responsibility for Reporting Materials – As a user of the family computer network you have a responsibility to report threatening or obscene materials, expressions of racism or hate, or other materials which are intended to embarrass, harass or cause harm to you, a family member or any other individual, to your parents. Your parents have the right to delete, read, or take other appropriate action with regard to such materials reported or discovered on your computer or workstation.

8. Responsibility with Respect to Created Materials – As a user of the family computer network you have a responsibility to NOT knowingly transmit, duplicate, or distribute any materials, which are not in compliance with the terms and conditions of this Internet usage policy.

Protecting your Internet Child at School

You do everything right at home. You've created a safe Internet environment for your children. You've discussed Internet access with the parents of your children's friends. You've become reasonably assured that your child will be as safe as possible while accessing the Internet, either at home or at a friend's home.

Most people would stop worrying at this point. Many parents don't even think of Internet access at school. They naively assume the schools Internet access is safe, after all they deal with children every day and everyone is so sure the school has the children's best interest in mind. This is not always the case, granted many public schools that do offer Internet access, do provide reasonable security. However, there are many smaller public and private schools that may not have the budget, or the knowledge to install such tools.

Does the School offer Internet access

Many schools are beginning to provide teachers and students Internet access. Corporations and governments are spending millions to provide computer equipment to schools.

Schools are putting class schedules and assignments online to make it easier for parents and students. The problem starts when they spend money to place technology into the classroom but fail to provide proper training, and security procedures. Without adequate training and monitoring programs this technology quickly becomes a focus of concern, and instead of helping students, they become victims.

Does the school have an acceptable use policy

The first thing you need to do is contact your child's school and simply ask if they have internet access. If they do not have Internet access, then inform the school to notify you when they do get Internet Access.

If they do have Internet access, then ask if they have an acceptable use policy for both students and staff. You will also want to ask if they have adequate filtering software, that effectively filters all connections to the Internet, this includes students and staff members.

It is also advisable that you join your child's Parent Teacher Association and discuss with the PTA what assurances the school has made to protect your child.

I have found reports of school that have no filtering software at all. The school claims that it is not necessary because the children do not have access to the internet as it is only for the use of the school staff.

Some may think this is fine, but I don't! Without adequate filtering software, teachers have no idea what could popup during a web search on their classroom computer, if a child should happen to be at the teacher's desk when less than desirable images popup, then the damage is done.

Tracking User Activity

If your child's school does offer Internet access to the students, then each child should be assigned a user name and password. The school should then provide that user name and password to the students parents.

Simply having the user name and password is not enough. Make sure the school provides regular reports of your child's Internet activity while using the school network. If the school won't offer regular reports, at least verify that they can provide such a report upon request.

In the event of a problem such as a missing child, this type of report could be invaluable in locating the child.

Internet Filtering

Even if your child's school does offers Internet access to the student, and they have filtering software, then be aware that Internet filtering software is not 100 percent effective, and incidents will happen. The school administrators, students, teachers and parents need to understand that with Internet access there is a level of risk involved.

Discuss with the school staff how they expect to handle these incidents, and what plans are in place to handle such a situation. If there is no policy in place, then bring the topic to light at the next PTA meeting, and encourage the PTA to actively work with the school administration to establish a policy.

Who to Call

First and foremost, if a child is in immediate physical danger, call 911.

If your child does receive sexually explicit images from an online correspondent, or if he or she is solicited sexually, contact your local police.

Additionally, you should contact the Congressionally mandated CyberTipline. The CyberTipLine is a reporting mechanism for cases of child sexual exploitation including child pornography, online enticement of children for sex acts, molestation of children outside the family, sex tourism of children, child victims of prostitution, and unsolicited obscene material sent to a child. Reports may be made 24-hours per day, 7 days per week online at:

www.cybertipline.com

or by calling

1-800-843-5678

In Canada, you should contact your local police. You may also report the incident to the CyberTip hotline at:

www.cybertip.ca

The Internet Crime Complaint Center

The Internet Crime Complaint Center is a partnership between the Federal Bureau of Investigation, (FBI), and the National White Collar Crime Center.

The Internet Crime Complaint Centers mission is to serve as a vehicle to receive, develop, and refer criminal complaints regarding the rapidly expanding arena of cyber crime. The Internet Crime Complaint Center gives the victims of cyber crime a convenient and easy-to-use reporting mechanism that alerts authorities of suspected criminal or civil violations.

For law enforcement and regulatory agencies at the federal, state, local and international level, the Internet Crime Complaint Center provides a central referral mechanism for complaints involving Internet related crimes.

Conclusion

Physical Supervision and open communication are key elements to protecting your Internet Child. Nothing else can beat it! As I stated early, placing the computer in a public location such as the kitchen or family room makes it easy to keep an eye on what your kids are doing online.

Talking to your children, and making sure they know and understand the rules and the consequences of breaking those rules, will go a long way in protecting them. They should also know that you have the tools and the knowledge to keep track of their Internet usages.

The Internet has made our world much smaller, and that's not necessarily a bad thing. Children today have the opportunity to speak to other children all over the world, to exchange points of view and opinions with someone from another culture, to learn and understand other people and their customs and to learn to respect peoples' differences.

With a smaller world, those bent on preying on others also find it easier to find victims. Spammers have found a more economical way to attract customers, and many of those spammers have no regard for decency.

Software tools are great, and in many cases are an adequate method to controlling web content and what your children can see or do online. $39.95 may be a small price to pay for software to protect your children, but ultimately, they are your responsibility, and software is not perfect. You as a parent, must be diligent is monitoring your child's Internet activity.

Bibliography

Donna Rice Hughes
http://www.protectkids.com

Federal Bureau of Investigation - Cyber Division
http://www.fbi.gov/publications/pguide/pguidee.htm

National Academy of Sciences
http://www.nap.edu/netsafekids/pp_sp.html

Perverted Justice
http://www.perverted-justice.com

Purdue University
http://www.educause.edu

Wauconda Area Public Library District
http://www.wauclib.org/Policies/internetpolicy.html

Little Rock Kids
http://www.littlerockkids.com/parents/safety/internet.html

Federal Trade Commission
http://www.ftc.gov/privacy/privacyinitiatives/childrens.html

TechGenix Ltd
http://www.windowsecurity.com/whitepaper/Email_Harvesti
ng_Techniques_FAQ.html

Media Awareness Network
http://www.bewebaware.ca/english/OnlinePredators.aspx

Bibliography

National Center for Missing & Exploited Children
http://www.missingkids.com/cybertip

Carnegie Mellon University
http://www.cert.org/tech_tips/home_networks.html

Wired Kids
http://www.wiredsafety.org/safety/index.html

Wikipedia
http://en.wikipedia.org/wiki/Main_Page

Glen Klinkhart
A Cyber Cops Guide to Internet Child Safety